Josephine Community Libraries
Grants Pass, Oregon

ƎISCARDEᴑ

American Heart

D0117725

'e SM

H E A R T S A V E R ®

P E D I A T R I C   F I R S T   A I D

W I T H   C P R   a n d   A E D

DATE DUE   1/14

APR 16 2015	
AUG 6 2015	
AUG 27 2015	
AUG 17 2017	
ƎISCARDEᴑ	

PRINTED IN U.S.A.

ISBN 0-87493-482-6

© 2006 American Heart Association

Contents

Josephine Community Libraries
Grants Pass, Oregon

CD Contents

Being Ready
   Child and Infant Safety Checklist
   First Aid Kit Suggested Contents

Preparing for Disasters
   Links to the Federal Emergency Management Agency (FEMA)

Reference Materials
   CPR/AED
      AHA Website Links
      Anatomy and Physiology: Understanding the Importance of CPR
      Choosing the Correct AED Pads or System
      CPR and AED Use—Legal and Ethical Issues
      CPR and AED Use—The Human Aspect
      Frequently Asked Questions (FAQs)
      Heart Attack and Stroke
      Taking Care of an AED
   First Aid
      Common Childhood Illnesses
      Coral Snakes
      General Groups of Poisons
      Map of Reported Cases of Lyme Disease
      Sample Medical Emergency Response Report
      US Americans With Disabilities Act and Child Care Centers

Video Clips
   Removing Gloves
   Finding the Problem
   Adult/Child Choking
   Infant Choking
   Stopping Bleeding
   Bandaging
   Splinting
   Adult CPR
   Child CPR
   Adult/Child AED
   Infant CPR

Preface

Children are our future, and the American Heart Association (AHA) is dedicated to protecting that future by delivering optimal education that teaches First Aid and CPR skills. With the basic First Aid you will learn in this course, you could make a difference in the lives of others. You might even save the life of someone you know.

The AHA infant and child Chain of Survival focuses on prevention of injuries and illnesses and early access to medical care.

Our Heartsaver Pediatric First Aid Course uses this pediatric Chain of Survival to teach students the basics of first aid, including injury prevention and when to get help if needed.

The members of the AHA First Aid Task Force have been instrumental in developing this course. Their outstanding efforts underscore their commitment to providing exceptional first aid education to people around the world.

William W. Hammill, MD

First Aid Task Force Chair

Considerations for International Readers

The following table is intended for international participants of this course. It is meant to help explain materials in this course that may be relevant only to those in the United States. For more specific information about your local practices and organizations please contact your instructor.

Page 5	The American Academy of Pediatrics website (*www.aap.org*) contains information about child health, safety, and development. This site contains some information specific to the United States.
Page 11	In the *NHTSA Proper Child Safety Seat Use Chart,* child weights are given in pounds and child heights are given in feet and inches. Please note the following metric conversions: For infants, 20 to 22 lb = 9 to 10 kg For toddlers, 20 lb = 9 kg; 40 lb = 18 kg For young children, 40 lb = 18 kg; 4′9″ = 1.4 m
Page 12	The US National Highway Transportation Safety Administration (NHTSA) website offers child safety seat information. This site contains information specific to the United States.
Page 13	This book refers to regulations particular to individual states within the United States. Contact your instructor or local authorities to learn more about safety regulations particular to your area.
Page 16	The US Federal Emergency Management Agency's (FEMA) website is listed on this page. This website contains information about disaster management specific to the United States.
Page 16	In the section **Access to Emergency Medical Service,** a telephone number is given for Poison Control within the United States. Please consult your instructor for the important emergency response numbers in your area.
Pages 18-19	The American National Standards Institute (ANSI) and the Occupational Safety and Health Administration (OSHA) are US organizations. Please consult your local authority's recommendations for the contents of first aid kits.
Page 21	Good Samaritan laws vary by country and locality. Please talk to your instructor to see which laws apply to your area.
Page 22	The Americans With Disabilities Act (ADA) is specific to the United States. Please contact your local authority for information about the protections for people with illnesses and disabilities in your area.
Page 24	The Occupational Safety and Health Administration (OSHA) is a US organization. Please contact your local authority for the safety and health standards for your workplace.
Page 43	The website *www.betterasthmacare.org* contains information about medications and practices relating to asthma that are specific to the United States. Please consult your instructor about common medications and practices for asthma in your area.
Page 74	The black widow spider and the brown recluse spider are given as examples of poisonous spiders. These spiders are native to the United States. Please talk to your instructor about poisonous insects and spiders in your area.
Page 80	**NOTE:** In the section **Poison Control Center Contact Information,** the telephone number for the US National Poison Control Center (800-222-1222) is for the US only. Please ask your instructor for the poison control number in your area.
Page 98	In step 5 of the section **Actions for Chest Compressions,** please note the following metric conversion: 1½ to 2 inches = 4 to 5 cm

Introduction

Overview

Caring for children is a pleasure and a duty. This book tries to help make that duty easier.

This student workbook gives you first aid basics for children. As you use this student workbook, remember that you don't have to make all the decisions. We will tell you how to get help if you need it.

Who Should Take This Course

We created this course for anyone who needs to learn basic first aid, including child care workers, teachers, parents, grandparents, and volunteers who work with children.

How This Course Is Organized

You will learn first aid basics through this student workbook and the video for the course. After each section of the course, you will answer a few written test questions and discuss the answers with your instructor.

During the course you will practice some skills. If you demonstrate that you can do the skills taught in the course, you will receive a Heartsaver Pediatric First Aid card.

Josephine Community Libraries
Grants Pass, Oregon

Using This Student Workbook

This student workbook is both a classroom textbook and a workbook. You should use this student workbook in the following ways:

When	Then you should
Before the course	• Read this student workbook and look at the pictures on each page. • Watch the video clips on the CD. This will help you learn the important points and prepare for practice during the course.
During the course	• Use this student workbook to understand the important information and skills taught in the course. • Take notes about your group's policies and procedures. For example, if you work in a facility that has established policies and procedures for emergencies, review these documents and take notes about how this information will apply to you.
After the course	• Review the skills frequently. Look at the practice sheets in the student workbook or the video skills on the CD. This will help you remember the steps of first aid, CPR, and automated external defibrillator (AED) use. You'll always be ready if there is an emergency.

Using the Student CD

More information is available on the Heartsaver Pediatric First Aid CD (included with this student workbook). You should use the student CD in the following ways:

When	Then you should
Before the course	• Watch the video clips. This will help you learn the important points and prepare for practice during the course.
After the course	• View the video clips after class as a review. • Review the reference materials and other information on the CD.

See the list of CD contents inside the front cover of this student workbook.

Heartsaver Pediatric First Aid Quick Reference Guide

The Heartsaver Pediatric First Aid Quick Reference Guide summarizes first aid actions for many injuries and illnesses. Use this to help you remember how to give first aid after you take this course.

How Often Training Is Needed

Review your student workbook, student CD, and quick reference guide often to keep your skills fresh. You need to retake this course every 2 years to get a new course completion card.

Icons

These icons will help you as you use this student workbook.

Icon	Meaning
	This information is for schools and child care centers.
	Go online for more information about this topic.
	Check the student CD for more information about this topic.
Regs	Check your regulatory agency for details about this topic.

How to Interact With Children of Different Ages

What You Will Learn

By the end of this section you should be able to

- Tell how to interact with infants
- Tell how to interact with toddlers
- Tell how to interact with young children
- Tell how to interact with adolescents
- Tell how to interact with children who have special needs

Overview

Children at different developmental stages react to situations differently. Children of different ages require different types of care. For example, when you are caring for a newborn baby, you must support her neck when you hold her. You must also protect the infant because she can't protect herself or tell you what is wrong.

This is very different from caring for an 8-year-old boy who can protect his body but also can place his body at risk (eg, walking out into the street). The 8-year-old can also tell you how he feels.

For more information on how children develop, visit the American Academy of Pediatrics website: *www.aap.org*.

FYI: Developmental Age vs Real Age

Children who are ill, injured, or afraid often do not act their age. Instead, they may act like a younger child. Treat ill, injured, or frightened children based on their behavior, not their age.

The table on the next page explains the characteristics and interaction tips for children of different ages.

Category	Age	Characteristics	Interaction Tips

Infants	**Birth to 1 year**	• Infants less than 4 months of age may not be able to hold head up
		• Cannot talk
		• Cry to tell you they are
		  — Hungry
		  — Tired
		  — Wet
		  — Lonely
		  — Scared
		  — Hurt
			• Support the head when you lift or carry an infant less than 4 months of age.
			• Use a soft, quiet voice when you talk to an infant.
			• Use gentle motions when you approach an infant.
			• Keep the infant warm but not overly hot.

Toddlers	**1 to 3 years**	• Learning to talk
		• Active, moving around and making noise
		• May bite other children when frustrated
		• A toddler who is not active or is acting differently than usual may be
		  — Sick
		  — Hurt
		  — Afraid
		  — Tired
			• Toddlers may not speak well.
			• They can often understand what others say.
			• They may be afraid of adults they do not know.
			• You may need to give extra comfort when a healthcare provider arrives to care for a toddler.

Young Children	**4 to 10 years**	• Developmental stages overlap greatly within this age group • Often pick up on the feelings of adults around them • Can understand simple explanations • Fear separation from caregivers and friends	• Stay calm. • Use simple words to tell young children what is happening.

Category	Age	Characteristics	Interaction Tips

Adolescents	**11 to 18 years**	• Understand almost everything around them
		• Often act without worrying about consequences of their actions
		• May take risks such as experimenting with drugs, alcohol, and driving cars
		• May worry about
		  — How others view them
		  — Whether an injury will be permanent
		  — Getting into trouble because of an injury
		• May not share information with a first aid rescuer and especially the adolescent's own parent or guardian
			• Tell them what you are doing to help them.
			• Reassure them without talking down to them.

Children With Special Needs	**Any age**	• Have physical, mental, or emotional needs that require special care	• Work with family members or other caregivers to know how to use medical devices or medicines.

Child Safety

What You Will Learn

By the end of this section you should be able to

- Understand the importance of preventing injuries before they occur:
    — At home
    — In and around a car
    — On the playground or sports field
    — At a child care facility
    — Around water
- List how to prevent injuries at home
- Tell how to reduce the risk of SIDS

Overview

It would be wonderful if children did not have any injuries. But we all know that injuries do happen. Preventing injuries is the first link in the AHA infant and child Chain of Survival.

Most Common Injuries in Children

Injuries are the most common cause of death from 1 to 44 years of age. This year a child you know will probably be injured seriously enough to require emergency care. Injuries are often thought to be "accidents" that can't be avoided. But at least half of fatal injuries can be prevented by simple actions in the home, car, child care center, school, and playground.

The most common fatal childhood injuries that can be prevented are

- Motor vehicle passenger injuries
- Pedestrian injuries
- Bicycle injuries
- Drowning
- Burns
- Firearm injuries

Safety at Home

The average home can be a dangerous place for children. Parents can work to make a home safe for children. Here are some things you can do to make the home safer.

■ Post your emergency response number (or 911), the poison control center number, and the child's healthcare provider's number near a phone where you keep other important information.

■ Keep children away from things that can hurt them.

Item	Action
Electrical outlets	Cover with protective covers
Medicine	Store in locked cabinets away from children's reach
Knives and sharp objects	Keep out of children's reach
Hot stove tops, burners, and ovens	Use stove guards and keep children away
Cleaning supplies	Store on high shelves or in locked cabinets
Stairs	Use stair gates or guards to keep toddlers from climbing or falling
Firearms	Unload and store in a locked cabinet

■ Install smoke and carbon monoxide detectors.

■ Install window guards to keep windows from opening completely.

■ Make sure that the house or apartment number is visible from the street in case emergency personnel need to find it.

Do Not
NEVER shake a baby. Shaking or tossing a baby in the air while playing can cause serious injury.

Car Safety

Children and cars can be a dangerous combination. You must use extra care with children in and around cars:

■ Make sure everyone in the car (including the driver) uses seat belts at all times. Infants and young children should be belted in an appropriate child safety seat.

■ Keep children from sticking their arms or heads out the window while someone is driving.

■ Use a child safety lock on car doors, if available, when driving young children.

■ Keep young children from playing with automatic window controls or automatic van doors.

■ Never leave a child alone in a car.

Child Safety Seats

Child safety seats that meet your state's safety guidelines have been shown to help keep children safe.

The following table shows the guidelines from the National Highway Traffic Safety Association (NHTSA) for using child safety seats in vehicles.

NHTSA Proper Child Safety Seat Use Chart

	Infants	**Toddlers**	**Young Children**
Weight	Birth to 1 year old and up to 20 lb	Over 1 year and over 20 lb, up to 40 lb	Ages 4 to 8 and over 40 lb unless taller than 4´9˝
Type of Seat	Infant only or rear-facing convertible	Convertible or forward-facing	Seatbelt-positioning booster seat
Seat Position	Rear-facing only	Forward facing	Forward facing
Always Make Sure	Children under 1 year old and under 20 lb should be in rear-facing seats. Harness straps should be at or below shoulder level.	Harness straps should be at or above shoulders. Most forward-facing seats require top slot for seatbelt.	Seatbelt-positioning booster seats must be used with both lap and shoulder belt. The lap belt should fit low and tight across the child's lap or upper thigh area, and the shoulder belt should fit snugly, crossing the chest and shoulder to avoid abdominal injuries.
	All children 12 years of age and younger should sit in the back seat.		

Not all child safety seats fit well in all vehicles. If you provide child care and plan to transport children, use only child safety seats that are appropriate for your vehicle. Some child safety seats are more standard in design to fit most vehicles. Parents and caregivers should transport children in their care with the appropriate child safety seats.

For more information on child safety seats, visit www.nhtsa.gov.

> ### *Important: Children and Shoulder Belts*
>
> The shoulder belt should not cross the child's neck. If it does, lower the harness or put the child in a seatbelt-positioning child safety seat.

Installing a Child Safety Seat

A child safety seat is safe only if you have installed it properly. Learn how to properly install the safety seat. In your community you may find child passenger safety experts in some or all of the following places:

- Fire station
- Police department
- Local emergency medical service
- Highway patrol
- Hospital
- Insurance company

Visit the NHTSA website to locate a child passenger safety inspection station in your area: *www.nhtsa.gov/cps/cpsfitting*.

Traffic Safety

When children are near traffic

- Children should learn to hold hands with adults when in a parking lot or crossing a street.
- Children should "stop, look, and listen" before crossing a street at a corner, with a traffic light, or at a stop sign.
- Children walking on a sidewalk should watch for cars that are backing out of driveways or exiting parking lots.

On the Playground or Sports Field

Many childhood injuries happen on the playground and while children are playing organized sports. To prevent some of these injuries

- Supervise young children when they are playing on a playground or participating in organized sports.
- Ensure that children wear closed-toe shoes when playing.
- Ensure that children wear all protective gear appropriate for the sport they are playing.
- Ensure that children wear bicycle helmets when riding a bike.
- Check the playground to ensure that it is safe and free of broken bottles and other harmful trash.

It is a good idea for parents/guardians to visit with a child's healthcare provider before the child starts to play a new organized sport to make sure the child is healthy enough to play.

At a Child Care Facility

Injury prevention is critical at child care facilities. Each state has specific safety rules that child care facilities must follow. Before you enroll your child, visit the facility.

Take the Child and Infant Safety Checklist on the student CD with you to make sure the facility is safe for your child.

 Check your state regulations for additional details.

Around Water

Swimming pools, creeks, fountains, lakes, and rivers are interesting to most children. Parents should be aware of the dangers posed by any body of water. What's more, infants and young children can drown in bathtubs, toilets, or buckets in only a few inches of water.

Remember these safety tips for children and water:

- Do not leave a child alone in a bathtub or near any water.
- Closely watch all children near pools or other bodies of water. A child is at risk for drowning even if the child knows how to swim.
- Always stay within reach of a child near a body of water.

 Check your state regulations for additional details.

13

Reducing the Risk of SIDS

According to the American Academy of Pediatrics, SIDS (sudden infant death syndrome) is the sudden death of an infant under 1 year of age that is not explained by other causes. SIDS is the leading cause of death in infants between 28 days and 11 months of age.

Sleeping Positions

Several years ago researchers learned that SIDS is more likely to occur in infants who sleep on their stomachs than in infants who sleep on their backs.

When putting an infant down to sleep, all parents and other persons responsible for the care of infants should lay a healthy infant on his or her back. *Remember:* Place the infant *"back to sleep."*

Objects to Avoid

To reduce the risk of SIDS, do not place infants to sleep

- With any loose blankets, sheets, quilts, comforters, bumper pads, or soft materials in the bed
- On soft materials such as lamb's wool, a fluffy comforter, or a waterbed
- With objects such as stuffed animals that might fall against the baby's face and make it hard for the baby to breathe

Child and Infant Safety Checklist

For more information on child safety, see the Child and Infant Safety Checklist on page 128.

First Aid Basics

What You Will Learn

By the end of this section you should be able to tell

- Why you might need an emergency response plan or first aid action plan
- What the emergency response number is

Overview

Some first aid rescuers are required to have an emergency response plan. It is usually a good idea for most schools, workplaces, and even families to prepare for emergencies and first aid responses.

First Aid Action Plan

A first aid action plan is a written plan for medical, injury, and environmental emergencies. It includes

- The emergency response number
- The location of the first aid kit
- Instructions such as
  - Names of people in your facility who have first aid training
  - Telephone numbers and locations of nearby emergency care facilities
  - Telephone number of the poison control center

Child care facilities and schools should have a record and first aid action plan for each child who has a medical issue that lists

- Medical history and medications
- How and when to give the medications
- How to reach parents
- The name and telephone number of the child's healthcare provider

Make sure you know where your facility stores medications. Also make sure the medicines are stored in a way that

- Protects the privacy of the child
- Keeps unauthorized children and adults from access

Emergency Response Plan

It is important to have an emergency response plan for potential dangers in your area. This may also be called a disaster plan. For example, if you live in a coastal area, have a plan for hurricane emergencies.

Have a plan that includes

- How to escape a home or building
- Where to go in the building in case of an emergency
- How to access emergency medical services

Have regular drills to practice your emergency response plans.

Visit *http://fema.gov* for sample emergency response plans for different emergencies and natural disasters.

Access to Emergency Medical Service

At times you will need to phone your emergency response number (or 911) for help. Make sure you know your phone system. Do you need to dial 9 to get an outside line before you dial your emergency response number (or 911)? Know this *before* you need to phone for help. Put this instruction in your first aid action plan and your emergency response plan.

Write emergency numbers in a central location with the telephone, including your emergency response number (or 911) and the number for the poison control center (800-222-1222).

> ### *Your Emergency Response Number*
>
> If there is an emergency in this area, phone _____
> (fill in the blank).

Phoning for Help

This section includes general rules for phoning for help. Your organization may have specific rules about when you should phone your emergency response number.

Reasons to Phone for Help

As a general rule, you should phone your emergency response number (or 911) and ask for help whenever

- Someone is seriously ill or hurt
- You are not sure what to do in an emergency

Remember: It is better to phone for help even if you might not need it than not to phone when someone does need help.

How to Phone for Help

The following table shows how to phone for help:

If you are	Then you should
Alone	<ul><li>Yell for help while you start to check the child.</li><li>If no one answers your yell and immediate care isn't needed<ul><li>— Leave the child for a moment while you phone your emergency response number (or 911).</li><li>— Get the first aid kit and automated external defibrillator (AED) if available.</li></ul></li><li>Return to the child.</li></ul>
With other adults	<ul><li>Stay with the child and be ready to give first aid or start the steps of CPR if you know how.</li><li>Send someone else to phone your emergency response number (or 911) and get the first aid kit and AED if available.</li></ul>

Answering Dispatcher Questions

When you phone your emergency response number (or 911), be prepared to answer some questions about the emergency. Here are some sample questions that an emergency response dispatcher may ask you:

- "Where is your emergency and what number are you calling from?"
- "What is the emergency?"
- "What is your name?"
- "Is the victim conscious?"
- "Is the victim breathing normally?"
- "Are you able to assist with CPR?"
- "Do you have access to an AED?"

Do not hang up until the dispatcher tells you to do so.

FYI: Emergency Dispatchers

When you phone for help, the emergency dispatcher may be able to tell you how to do CPR, give first aid, or use an AED.

First Aid Kits

A first aid kit has many of the supplies you might need when giving first aid to an injured or ill child.

Suggested Contents for a First Aid Kit

Not all first aid kits contain the same supplies. The American National Standards Institute (ANSI) recommends that the materials below be in a first aid kit. OSHA refers to this ANSI list in their regulations.

Consider keeping the items listed below in your first aid kit.

The CD has a first aid kit list you can modify for your home first aid kit or to meet childcare regulations.

Suggested Contents for First Aid Kits

Item	Minimum Size or Volume	Quantity per package	Unit package size
List of important local emergency telephone numbers, including police, fire department, EMS, and poison control center			
Absorbent compress*	32 sq. in.	1	1
Adhesive bandage*	1″ x 3″	16	1
Adhesive tape*	5 yd. (total)	1 or 2	1 or 2
Antibiotic treatment*	1/32 oz.	6	1
Antiseptic swab*	0.14 fl. oz.	10	1
Antiseptic wipe*	1″ x 1″	10	1
Antiseptic towlette*	24 sq. in.	10	1
Bandage compress (2 in.)*	2″ x 36″	4	1
Bandage compress (3 in.)*	3″ x 60″	2	1
Bandage compress (4 in.)*	4″ x 72″	1	1
Burn dressing*	4″ x 4″	1	1 or 2
Burn treatment*†	1/32 oz.	6	1
CPR barrier*		1	1 or 2
Cold pack (4″ x 5″)*	4″ x 5″	1	2
Eye covering, with means of attachment (2.9 sq. in.)*	2.9 sq. in.	2	1
Eye wash*	1 fl. oz. total	1	2
Eye wash and covering, with means of attachment (1 fl. oz. total, 2.9 sq. in.)*	1 fl. oz. total 2.9 sq. in.	1 2	2
Gloves*		2 pair	1 or 2

Item	Minimum Size or Volume	Quantity per package	Unit package size
Roller bandage (4 in.)*	4″ x 6 yd.	1	1
Roller bandage (2 in.)*	2″ x 6 yd.	2	1
Sterile pad*	3″ x 3″	4	1
Triangular bandage*	40″ x 40″ x 56″	1	1
Heartsaver Pediatric First Aid Quick Reference Guide			1

*Items meet the ANSI Z308.1-2003 standard.
†Do not put ointment on a burn unless a healthcare provider tells you to do so.

Some regulatory agencies require that you keep a thermometer, eye protection, or other supplies in a first aid kit.

 For details check with the regulatory agency that oversees your child care facility.

Automated External Defibrillator

Some schools, businesses, and other public places have an automated external defibrillator (AED). The AED is a machine with a computer inside. An AED can

- Recognize cardiac arrest that requires a shock
- Tell the rescuer when a shock is needed
- Give a shock if needed

You will learn more about AEDs later in this student workbook.

It is important to keep your first aid kit close to the AED and a phone. This way you can quickly phone your emergency response number (or 911) and have all the supplies you need ready for use in an emergency (Figure 1).

Figure 1. Write the emergency response number on a big sign in the first aid kit and on a large sign near the telephone.

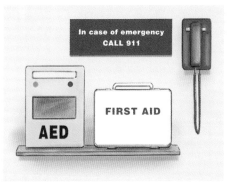

Learning Objectives

By the end of this section you should be able to

- Tell what first aid is
- Tell who has a duty to give first aid
- Explain your role in keeping first aid care confidential

What First Aid Is

First aid is the immediate care you give someone with an illness or injury *before* trained help arrives and takes over. For example

- For minor illnesses and injuries like a minor scrape, you might apply a bandage.
- For serious illnesses and injuries, such as a broken bone, you will care for the child until trained help arrives and takes over. Trained help could be someone whose job is taking care of people who are ill or injured such as an EMS responder, nurse, or doctor.

Responsibility to Provide First Aid

Some people, such as police officers, have a duty to respond. Other people do not, even if they have first aid training. If you do not have a duty to respond and you drive past a car crash, *you* can decide whether to stop and help. If you walk down the street and see a person who seems ill, *you* can decide if you will help.

An adult can refuse care, but a child under 18 years of age cannot. If a child needs first aid and you are required to give first aid as part of your job responsibilities, you must give it unless the child's parent or legal guardian has given you instructions not to give first aid to the child. In that case, phone your emergency response number (or 911), and stay with the child until trained help arrives and takes over.

The following shows when someone *must give first aid:*
- When giving first aid is part of your job responsibilities or job description **and**
- When the injury or illness happens during your working hours

But even people with a duty to respond can decide whether to stop and help when they are off duty.

Duty to Act

When you give first aid, you have a legal responsibility to act the way a reasonable person with your level of training would act.

No one expects you to give the level of care given by a professional such as an emergency medical service (EMS) rescuer, a nurse, a physician, or other health-care worker.

Liability and Ethics

It is critical that you try to prevent injuries before they happen.

Adults can decide about their health care and whether they want to receive first aid. This is not true for children. If you must give first aid as part of your job requirement, remember that you *must* give first aid to a child unless the child's parent or legal guardian has given you instructions not to do so.

Good Samaritan Act

Good Samaritan laws generally protect the first aid rescuer from liability. The law assumes that first aid rescuers act in good faith and within the limits of their first aid training. Each state has some form of Good Samaritan law.

Confidentiality

As a first aid rescuer, you *must* protect the privacy of those to whom you give first aid.

The following table tells when to treat information confidentially:

You may share details with	You may not share details with
• Authorized healthcare provider(s) • Child's parents or legal guardians • Other legal authorities such as police or child protective services • Co-workers (how the injury happened and not necessarily the child's identity)	• Your friends • Your family • Parents of other children

Injury Report

If your organization requires it, you may have to file an injury report. This may include

- Personal information about the child
- How the injury occurred
- Anything you did to care for the child before trained help arrived

The Americans With Disabilities Act (ADA) has rules that protect people with serious illnesses and disabilities. Public businesses, schools, and privately run child care centers must comply with parts of the ADA.

Regs Check your state regulations for additional details.

For more information on child care centers and the ADA, visit the ADA website at *www.ada.gov*.

What You Will Learn

By the end of this section you should be able to

- Tell how to keep yourself safe when giving first aid
- Tell how to keep the child from further injury when giving first aid
- Show how to put on and take off protective gloves

Overview

The first step in first aid is to check the scene to make sure you and the sick or injured child are safe before you give first aid.

Scene Safety

The following describes how to make sure the scene is safe:

- Stop and look at the scene as you approach the child. Watch for special situations:
  - If a power line is down, stay away from it.
  - Do not walk through deep floodwater because there may be strong undercurrents.
- Look out for oncoming traffic. Ask others to direct traffic around the area (Figure 2).
- Before you start giving first aid, make sure you and the child are out of harm's way.
- If the scene is dangerous, move the child to a safer location. (See the section titled "Moving a Child" below.)

Figure 2. Ask others to direct traffic and phone your emergency response number.

Moving a Child

The only time you should move an injured child is if the scene is unsafe for you or the child or if the child is face down and needs CPR. Examples of unsafe places include a busy street or parking lot; near a fire, smoke, or gas; or in water.

FYI: Know Your Limits

When you give first aid, know your limits. Don't become another victim. Sometimes your wish to help can put you in danger. For example, if you are not a good swimmer, you must be very careful when you try to save a drowning child.

Using Personal Protective Equipment

Body fluids, such as blood, saliva, and urine, can sometimes carry germs that cause disease. Personal protective equipment includes gloves, masks, and eye protection. Personal protective equipment helps protect you from these body fluids and prevents the spreading of germs.

At home when giving first aid to family members, you may choose not to use personal protective equipment. But when you give first aid to other children, you should use personal protective equipment if possible (Figure 3). In this student workbook we use the phrase "if appropriate" to remind you to use personal protective equipment if your job requires it.

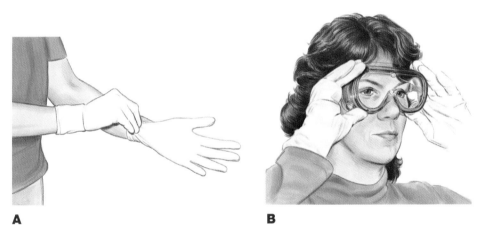

A **B**

Figure 3. A, Wear protective gloves whenever you give first aid, and **B,** wear eye protection if a child is bleeding.

What to Use When Personal Protective Equipment Is Required

For those who are required to use personal protective equipment, such as teachers and child care workers, you need the following equipment:

- Gloves to protect your hands from blood and other body fluids
- Eye protection, if the child is bleeding, to protect your eyes from blood and other body fluids
- Mask to protect you when you give breaths

The Occupational Safety and Health Administration (OSHA) and state regulatory agencies require that anyone who provides first aid as part of his job responsibilities must use personal protective equipment.

 Check with your state licensing agency for details.

How to Take Off Protective Gloves

When you give first aid, the outside of your gloves may touch blood or other body fluids. Take your gloves off without touching the outside of the gloves with your bare hands. Follow these steps to take off your gloves and see Figure 4:

Step	Action
1	Grip one glove on the *outside* of the glove near the cuff and peel it down until it comes off inside out.
2	Cup it with your other (gloved) hand.
3	Place 2 fingers of your bare hand *inside* the cuff of the glove that is still on your hand.
4	Peel that glove off so that it comes off *inside out* with the first glove inside it.
5	If there is blood on the gloves, dispose of the gloves properly: • Put them in a biohazard waste bag if required to do so by your workplace (Figure 5). • If you are at home and do not have a biohazard waste bag, put the gloves in a plastic bag that can be sealed before you dispose of it.
6	Wash your hands after you give first aid so that you don't spread germs. Wash your hands with soap and water as soon as you can. Use a waterless hand sanitizer if you do not have immediate access to soap and water.

Figure 4. Proper removal of protective gloves—without touching the outside of the gloves with your bare hands.

A. Grip outside of glove near cuff.

B. Peel glove down so it comes off inside out.

C. Place fingers of bare hand inside cuff of other glove.

D. Peel second glove so that it comes off inside out with first glove inside it.

Figure 5. Place all disposable equipment that has touched body fluids in a biohazard waste bag if one is available, and seal it. Don't throw the biohazard waste bag in the trash.

FYI: Latex Allergies

Some rescuers and victims may be allergic to latex. Use protective gloves that don't contain latex, for example vinyl gloves, whenever possible.

If you or the victim has a latex allergy, do not use gloves that contain latex.

If you have a latex allergy, tell your emergency response program supervisor and your Heartsaver Pediatric First Aid instructor before you start the course.

Hand Washing

Hand washing is the most important step in preventing illness. Follow these guidelines for washing hands:

- Wash your hands after you give first aid so that you don't spread germs.
- Use waterless hand sanitizers if you do not have immediate access to soap and water. Wash your hands with soap and water as soon as you can (Figure 6).

Figure 6. Wash your hands well with soap and water after giving first aid.

Disposing of Trash With Body Fluids

Not all places have biohazard bags. The following table tells you how to throw out disposable equipment that has touched body fluids:

With a biohazard bag	Without a biohazard bag
• Put the disposable equipment that has touched body fluids in the bio-hazard bag. • Seal the biohazard bag. • Don't throw the bag in the trash. • Instead, follow your group's plan for disposing of biohazardous waste.	• Talk with EMS personnel or your local hospital about how to throw out anything with blood on it.

Checking the Child for Injuries and Illnesses

Learning Objectives

By the end of this section you should be able to show how to find out what the problem is when a child is sick or hurt.

Overview

You must find out if the child is injured or ill. This is the first step when you give first aid.

How to Find Out What the Problem Is

After you check the scene to be sure it is safe, you must find out what the problem is before you give first aid. Learn to look for problems in order of importance. First look for problems that may be life-threatening. Then look for other problems.

Steps to Find the Problem

The following steps will help you find out what the problem is. They are listed in order of importance, with the most important step listed first.

Step	Action
1.	When you arrive at the scene, check the scene to be sure it is safe. As you walk toward the child, try to **look for signs of the cause of the problem.**
2.	Check whether the child responds. **Tap the child and shout, "Are you OK?"** (Figure 7). • A victim who "responds" will react in some way to your voice or touch. But remember that a child who responds now may stop responding, so you have to keep rechecking. — A child who responds and is awake may be able to answer your questions. Tell the child you are there to help and ask what the problem is. — A child may only be able to move or just moan or groan when you tap him and shout. If so, phone or send someone to phone your emergency response number (or 911) and get the first aid kit. • A child who "does not respond" does not move or react in any way when you tap him. Phone or send someone to phone your emergency response number (or 911) and get the first aid kit and AED.
3.	**Next, open the airway with a head tilt–chin lift if needed** (Figure 8). • If a child responds and is awake, the child is breathing. You will not need to open the airway. • If the child does not respond or only moans or groans, you have to open the airway before you can check whether the child is breathing: — Tilt the head by pushing back on the forehead. — Lift the chin by putting your fingers on the bony part of the chin. Do not press the soft tissues of the neck or under the chin. — Lift the chin to move the jaw forward.
4.	**Check whether the child is breathing.** • Place your ear next to the child's mouth and nose. • **Look** to see whether the chest is moving. • **Listen** for breaths. • **Feel** for breaths on your cheek.
5.	**Next, look for any obvious signs of injury, such as bleeding, broken bones, burns, or bites.** (You will learn about each of these problems later.)
6.	**Finally, look for medical information jewelry** (Figure 9). This tells you if the child has a serious medical condition.

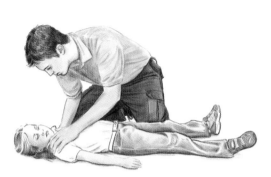

Figure 7. Check the child for injuries and illness before you give first aid.

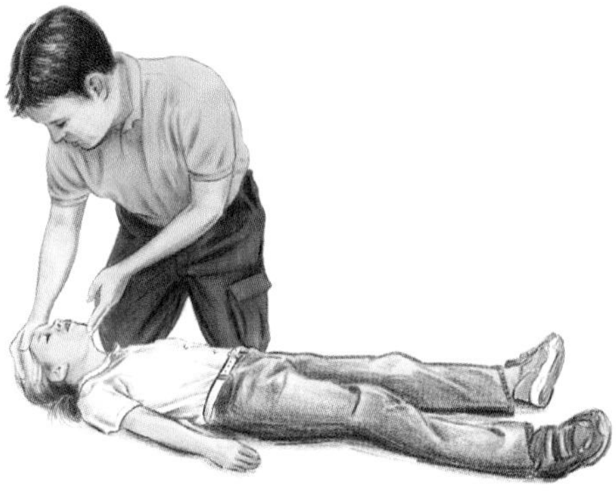

Figure 8. Open the child's airway with a head tilt–chin lift.

Figure 9. Look for medical information jewelry.

Important

Remember, a child's condition may change rapidly. A child may respond and then may stop responding, so check the child often.

When a child does not respond, the child may stop breathing. Watch carefully to make sure that the child keeps breathing. Be ready to give rescue breaths if the child stops breathing. (If you don't know how to do CPR and if you won't learn CPR in this course, you will learn how to give rescue breaths.)

Changing a Child's Position	Once you check the child for signs of injury and illness, you can decide whether you need to move the child into a different position.

The only time you should move an injured child is if the scene is unsafe for you or the child or if the child is facedown and needs CPR.

Managing Others While Caring for a Sick or Injured Child

Instructing Staff or Other Adults
Staff must keep the school or child care center running normally while you care for a sick or injured child. In other organizations, adults must help with other children while you care for the sick or injured child.

- If the child is sick, make sure your staff or another adult keeps all other children away from the sick child.
- If you need help caring for the child, send one staff member or adult to get the first aid kit while other staff or adults care for the other children.
- If necessary, tell a staff member or other adult to phone your emergency response number (or 911), the poison control center, a parent of the child who is ill or injured, or a healthcare provider.

Dealing With Parents
Parents will be very concerned if their child is injured or ill. You must be honest with the parents. Tell them as clearly as possible what happened.

- Be sure that you have correct telephone numbers for all parents so that you can contact them in an emergency.
- If this is a disaster or other emergency, give instructions to the children's parents based on your emergency response plan.
- If your school requires it, be sure to fill out an injury or accident report so that the parents know what happened and what first aid you gave.

Instructing Children
Children can tell when adults are stressed or worried. It is important to remain calm while caring for ill or injured children.

- Ask another adult to find an activity to keep the other children busy.
- If this is a disaster or other emergency, tell the children what to do based on your emergency response plan.

Rescue Breathing for Infants

What You Will Learn	By the end of this section you should be able to show how to give rescue breaths to an infant who does not respond and is not breathing.

Overview	If you don't know how to do CPR and if you won't learn CPR in this course, you will learn how to give rescue breaths.

Open the Airway

When giving rescue breaths you must give the infant breaths that make the chest rise. Before giving rescue breaths, you must open the airway with a head tilt–chin lift.

Performing the Head Tilt–Chin Lift

Follow these steps to perform a head tilt–chin lift:

Step	Action
1	Tilt the head by pushing back on the forehead. When tilting an infant's head, do not push it back too far because it may block the infant's airway.
2	Lift the chin by putting your fingers on the bony part of the chin. Do not press the soft tissues of the neck or under the chin.
3	Lift the chin to move the jaw forward.

Giving Breaths

Breaths are very important for infants who are not breathing or do not respond. Your breaths give oxygen to an infant who cannot breathe on his own.

If the infant is not breathing, you will have to give rescue breaths.

Actions for Giving Breaths

Follow these steps to give breaths to infants:

Step	Action
1	Hold the infant's airway open with a head tilt–chin lift.
2	Take a normal breath and cover the infant's mouth and nose with your mouth, creating an airtight seal.
3	Give a breath (blow for 1 second). Watch for chest rise as you give the breath (Figure 10).
4	If the chest does not rise, repeat the head tilt–chin lift.
5	Continue giving rescue breaths. Use "breath—one—two—breath—one—two" cycles until <ul><li>The infant starts breathing on his own</li><li>The infant starts moving on his own</li><li>You have given 20 rescue breaths</li></ul>
6	After you have given 20 breaths, or if the infant starts to respond, phone your emergency response number (or 911) if no one has done so.

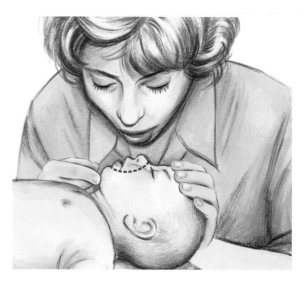

Figure 10. Giving breaths to an infant.

FYI: Tips for Giving Breaths

If your mouth is too small to cover the infant's nose and mouth, put your mouth over the infant's nose and give breaths through the infant's nose. (You may need to hold the infant's mouth closed to stop air from escaping through the mouth.)

Test Questions

Question	Your Notes
1. *True or false:* You should phone your emergency response number (or 911) and ask for help whenever someone is seriously ill or hurt or you are not sure what to do in an emergency. Circle your answer: True False	
2. *Fill in the blank with the correct word or words.* Children _____ years of age or younger should always be seated in the back seat of a car, with correct restraints for the child's size and age.	
3. *True or false* First aid is the care you give someone who is ill or injured before trained help arrives and takes over. Circle your answer: True False	

Question	Your Notes
4. *True or false* A teacher or child care worker can discuss giving first aid to a child with anyone. Circle your answer: True False	
5. *True or false* After you give first aid to a child, you should wash your hands so you don't spread germs. Circle your answer: True False	
6. *Fill in the blank with the correct word or words.* After you give first aid, you should put disposable equipment that has touched body fluids in a _____ bag if one is available.	
7. *True or false* After you check the scene to be sure it is safe, you should first look for problems that may be life-threatening. Circle your answer: True False	

Medical Emergencies

Breathing Problems

What You Will Learn	By the end of this section you should be able to

- List the signs of a child with a breathing problem
- Tell what to do when a child has a breathing problem
- Show how to relieve choking
- List the signs and actions for a child with a bad allergic reaction
- Show how to use an epinephrine pen

What Causes Breathing Problems

Body cells need oxygen to work properly. When you breathe, air goes down the air passages into the lungs. Oxygen then passes into the blood, which carries it to cells throughout the body.

The child may develop mild or severe block of the air passages by

- Something, such as food or some small object, going down "the wrong way" (into the air passages instead of the stomach)
- Swelling of the lining of the airway, for example, in a bad allergic reaction or severe asthma
- Infection
- Injuries to the head, neck, or chest

Signs of Breathing Problems

You can tell if someone is having trouble breathing if the person

- Is breathing very fast or very slowly
- Is having trouble with every breath
- Has noisy breathing—you hear a sound or whistle as air enters or leaves the lungs
- Doesn't have enough breath to make sounds or speak more than a few words at a time in between breaths although the person is trying to say more

Signs and Actions for Choking

When food or an object such as a toy gets in the airway, it can block the airway. Adults and children can easily choke while eating. Children can also easily choke when playing with small toys.

Choking can be a frightening emergency. If the block in the airway is severe, you must act quickly to remove the block. If you do, you can help the child breathe.

Use the following table to know whether a child is choking:

If the child	Then the block in the airway is	And you should
• Can make sounds • Can cough loudly	Mild	• Stand by and let the child cough • If you are worried about the child's breathing, *phone your emergency response number (or 911)*
• Cannot breathe • Has a cough that is very quiet or has no sound • Cannot talk or make a sound • Cannot cry (younger child) • Has high-pitched, noisy breathing • Has bluish lips or skin • Makes the choking sign	Severe	• Act quickly • Follow the steps below

FYI: The Choking Sign

A person who is choking may use the choking sign (holding the neck with one or both hands, Figure 11).

Figure 11. The choking sign. The person holds her neck with one or both hands.

How to Help a Choking Person Over 1 Year of Age

When a person is choking and suddenly cannot breathe, talk, or make any sounds, give abdominal thrusts. These thrusts are sometimes called the Heimlich maneuver. Abdominal thrusts push air from the lungs like a cough. This can help remove an object blocking the airway. You should give abdominal thrusts until the object is forced out and the person can breathe, cough, or talk or until the person stops responding.

Follow these steps to help a choking person who is 1 year of age and older:

Step	Action
1	If you think someone is choking, ask, "Are you choking?" If she nods, tell her you are going to help.
2	Kneel or stand firmly behind her and wrap your arms around her so that your hands are in front.
3	Make a fist with one hand.
4	Put the thumb side of your fist slightly above her navel (belly button) and well below the breastbone.
5	Grasp the fist with your other hand and give quick upward thrusts into her abdomen (Figure 12).
6	Give thrusts until the object is forced out and she can breathe, cough, or talk or until she stops responding.

Figure 12. Give quick upward thrusts into the child's abdomen.

Important

When abdominal thrusts are given to a choking victim, encourage the victim's parent or guardian to contact the child's healthcare provider.

Actions for a Choking Person Who Stops Responding

If you cannot remove the object, the victim will stop responding. When the victim stops responding, follow these steps:

Step	Action
1	Yell for help. If someone comes, send that person to phone your emergency response number (or 911) and get the AED if available.
2	Lower the victim to the ground, faceup. • If you are alone with the adult victim, phone your emergency response number (or 911) and get the AED. Then return to the victim and start the steps of CPR if you know how. (See "Adult CPR" on page 99.) • If you are alone with the child victim, start the steps of CPR if you know how. (See "Child CPR" on page 106.)
3	Every time you open the airway to give breaths, open the victim's mouth wide and look for the object (Figure 13). If you see an object, remove it with your fingers. If you do not see an object, keep giving sets of 30 compressions and 2 breaths until an AED arrives, the victim starts to move, or trained help arrives and takes over. Start the steps of CPR.
4	After about 5 cycles or 2 minutes, if you are alone, leave the child to call the emergency response number (or 911) and get the AED if available.
5	Return to the child and continue the steps of CPR if you know how.

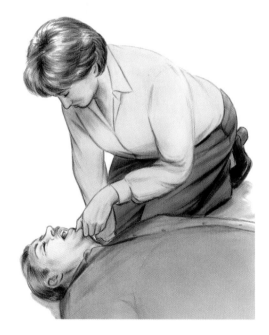

Figure 13. Open the mouth wide and look for an object.

FYI: Asking a Victim About Choking

Sometimes a victim is too young to answer your question or cannot answer your question for some other reason.

If the adult or child victim does not respond or cannot answer and you think the victim is choking, give abdominal thrusts until the object is forced out and the victim can breathe, cough, or talk or until the victim stops responding.

Actions to Help a Choking Large Person or Pregnant Woman

If the choking victim is in the late stages of pregnancy or is very large, use chest thrusts instead of abdominal thrusts (Figure 14).

Follow the same steps as above except for where you place your arms and hands. Put your arms under the victim's armpits and your hands on the center of the victim's chest. Pull straight back to give the chest thrusts.

Figure 14. Chest thrusts on a choking large person or pregnant woman.

How to Help a Choking Infant

When an infant is choking and suddenly cannot breathe or make any sounds, you must act quickly to help get the object out by using back slaps and chest thrusts.

Follow these steps to relieve choking in an infant:

Step	Action
1	Hold the infant facedown on your forearm. Support the infant's head and jaw with your hand. Sit or kneel and rest your arm on your lap or thigh.
2	Give up to 5 back slaps with the heel of your free hand between the infant's shoulder blades (Figure 15).
3	If the object does not come out after 5 back slaps, turn the infant onto his back. Move or open the clothes from the front of the chest only if you can do so quickly. You can push on the chest through clothes if you need to.
4	Give up to 5 chest thrusts using 2 fingers of your free hand to push on the breastbone in the same place you push for compressions (Figure 16): <ul><li>Support the head and neck.</li><li>Hold the infant with one hand and arm, resting your arm on your lap or thigh.</li></ul>
5	Alternate giving 5 back slaps and 5 chest thrusts until the object comes out and the infant can breathe, cough, or cry or until the infant stops responding.

Figure 15. Give up to 5 back slaps with the heel of your hand.

Figure 16. Give up to 5 chest thrusts.

When to Stop Back Slaps and Chest Thrusts

Stop back slaps and chest thrusts if

- The object comes out
- The infant begins to breathe, cough, or cry
- The infant stops responding

Actions for a Choking Infant Who Stops Responding

If you cannot remove the object, the infant will stop responding. When the infant stops responding, follow these steps:

Step	Action
1	Yell for help. If someone comes, send that person to phone your emergency response number (or 911).
2	Place the infant on a firm, flat surface. If possible, place the infant on a surface above the ground, such as a table. This makes it easier to give CPR to the infant.
3	Start the steps of CPR if you know how. (See "Infant CPR" on page 117.)
4	Every time you open the airway to give breaths, open the infant's mouth wide and look for the object. If you see an object, remove it with your fingers. If you do not see an object, keep giving sets of 30 compressions and 2 breaths. Continue CPR until the infant starts to move or trained help arrives and takes over.
5	After about 5 cycles or 2 minutes, if you are alone, leave the infant to call your emergency response number (or 911).
6	Return to the infant and continue the steps of CPR.

> **Do Not**
>
> *Do not* use abdominal thrusts on an infant. Abdominal thrusts could injure an infant.

Asthma

Asthma is common in children. It is a disease of the air passages. Air passages carry air to the lungs. During an asthma attack, a child may have

- Trouble breathing
- Coughing
- Tightness in the chest
- Wheezing (whistling-sounding)
- Fast breathing

Some children with asthma must take daily medication. Others take medicine only when they have asthma symptoms. Many children with asthma have an inhaler, which contains medicine that can make them feel better in a few minutes (Figure 17).

If a child with asthma has trouble breathing, even after medication, you may need to phone your emergency response number (or 911).

> ### *FYI: What Is a Spacer?*
>
> A spacer is a tool that fits on an inhaler and helps deliver the medicine more efficiently.

Figure 17. Some children with asthma may have a prescribed inhaler and spacer to help them take the right dose of medicine.

Actions for Asthma

Follow these steps if a child with asthma has an asthma attack:

Step	Action
1	Make sure that the scene is safe for you and the child.
2	Keep calm and soothe the child. Crying can make the asthma attack worse.
3	If the child has a prescription for asthma medicine, get the medicine and help the child take it.
4	Check the child's breathing. If the child is having trouble breathing, phone your emergency response number (or 911).
5	Be prepared to start CPR if the child stops breathing.
6	Stay with the child until trained help arrives and takes over.

Your day care center or school should have a first aid action plan for every child with asthma. If a child has an asthma attack, send another adult for the plan and the child's medicines.

 Check your state regulations for additional rules.

For more information on inhaled medications, you can view the State of California EMS Authority's "Asthma Care Training for Child Care Providers" video, in either English or Spanish, on the State of California EMS Authority website: *www.betterasthmacare.org.*

Allergic Reactions

Many allergic reactions are *mild,* but you should remember that *a mild allergic reaction can become a bad allergic reaction within minutes.*

FYI: Common Allergies

People can be allergic to many things, including

- Many foods, such as eggs, peanuts, chocolate
- Insect stings or bites, especially bee stings

Signs of Mild and Bad Allergic Reactions

The following table shows signs of mild and bad allergic reactions:

Mild Allergic Reaction	Bad Allergic Reaction
• A stuffy nose, sneezing, and itching around the eyes • Itching of the skin • Raised, red rash on the skin (hives) (Figure 18)	• Trouble breathing • Swelling of the tongue and face • Fainting

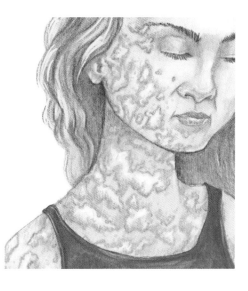

Figure 18. One sign of an allergic reaction can be a raised, red rash on the skin (hives).

Actions for Bad Allergic Reactions

A bad allergic reaction can be life-threatening and is an emergency. Follow these steps if you see signs of a *bad* allergic reaction:

Step	Action
1	Make sure the scene is safe.
2	Phone or send someone to phone your emergency response number (or 911) and get the first aid kit.
3	If the child is showing signs of a bad allergic reaction and has an epinephrine pen, ask the child to use it. (See the following section for instructions on how to use an epinephrine pen.)
4	If the child stops responding, start the steps of CPR if you know how (see the section on CPR).
5	If possible, save a sample of what caused the reaction. This may be helpful if this is the child's first allergic reaction.

Your day care center or school should have a first aid action plan for all children who have bad allergic reactions. If a child has a bad allergic reaction, send another adult for the plan and the child's medicines.

Children who carry epinephrine pens may know when and how to use them. An adult caring for a child with bad allergic reactions must know when and how to use an epinephrine pen. If the child cannot give the injection, you may help if you are trained and your state and workplace allow it.

Using an Epinephrine Pen

Some states and organizations permit first aid rescuers to help children use their epinephrine pen (see "How to Use an Epinephrine Pen").

An epinephrine pen is also called an epinephrine injector. It contains a small dose of medicine that can be injected through clothing (the side of the victim's leg). It will help someone with a bad allergic reaction breathe more easily. It usually takes several minutes before the medicine in the epinephrine pen starts to work.

 Check your local regulating body to know whether your state and organizations allow it.

How to Use an Epinephrine Pen

The epinephrine injection is given in the side of the thigh. There are 2 doses of epinephrine pens, one for adults and one for children. Make sure you have the epinephrine pen prescribed for that child.

Follow these steps to use an epinephrine pen:

Step	Action
1	Get the prescribed epinephrine pen.
2	Take off the safety cap (Figure 19A). Follow the instructions printed on the package.
3	Hold the epinephrine pen in your fist without touching either end because the needle comes out of one end.
4	Press the tip of the pen hard against the side of the child's thigh, about halfway between the hip and knee (Figure 19B). You can give the epinephrine pen directly to the skin or through clothing.
5	Hold the pen in place for several seconds. Some of the medication will remain in the pen after you use it.
6	Rub the injection spot for several seconds.
7	After using the epinephrine pen, follow your organization's policy for "sharps" disposal or give the pen to the EMS rescuers for proper disposal.
8	Write down the time of the injection. This information may be important for the trained help who cares for the child.
9	Stay with the child until trained help arrives and takes over.

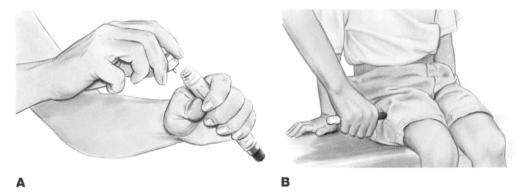

A **B**

Figure 19. Using an epinephrine pen. **A,** Take off the safety cap. **B,** Administer the epinephrine pen into the child's thigh (through clothing if necessary).

Diabetes and Low Blood Sugar

What You Will Learn

By the end of this section you should be able to

- Tell the signs of low blood sugar in a child with diabetes
- List the first aid actions for low blood sugar in a child with diabetes

What Causes Low Blood Sugar

Insulin in the body helps turn sugar into energy. Since people with diabetes do not make enough insulin, they may give themselves insulin injections. If a person with diabetes doesn't eat enough sugar for the amount of insulin injected, the sugar level in the blood drops. Low blood sugar causes the victim's behavior to change.

Low Blood Sugar

Low blood sugar can occur if a person with diabetes

- Has not eaten or has vomited
- Has not eaten enough food for the level of activity and amount of insulin already in the bloodstream
- Has injected too much insulin

Signs of Low Blood Sugar

Signs of low blood sugar can appear quickly and may include

- A change in behavior, such as confusion or irritability
- Sleepiness or even not responding
- Hunger, thirst, or weakness
- Sweating, pale skin color
- A seizure (see the section "Seizures")

Actions for Low Blood Sugar

Follow these steps if the child is *responding* and shows signs of low blood sugar:

Step	Action
1	If you have been trained, check the blood sugar level of a child with diabetes if the child is awake and alert but acts as if her blood sugar is low.
2	If you suspect or have confirmed that the blood sugar is low and the child can sit up and swallow, give the child something containing sugar to eat or drink.
3	Have the child sit quietly or lie down.
4	Phone or send someone to phone your emergency response number (or 911) if the child does not feel better within a few minutes after eating or drinking something containing sugar.
5	If you check the sugar and it is not low but the child is still not acting normally, phone the child's parents/guardians/healthcare provider or your emergency response number (or 911).

FYI: What to Give for Low Blood Sugar

The following shows what to give a child with diabetes who has low blood sugar:

- Fruit juice
- Packet of sugar or honey
- Non-diet soda
- Whatever the parent/guardian instructs you to give the child

Do **not** give foods that contain little or no sugar:

- Diet soda
- Chocolate
- Artificial sweetener

If the child *stops responding or is unable to sit up or swallow:*

Step	Action
1	Phone or send someone to phone your emergency response number (or 911).
2	Do not give the child anything to eat or drink. It may cause more harm.
3	If the child is having a seizure, follow the steps in the section on seizures. (See "Seizures" on the next page.)
4	If the child is not having a seizure and you do not suspect that the child has a head, neck, or spine injury, roll the child to his side to help keep the airway open.
5	If you have been trained to give the child his prescribed glucagon emergency kit, give it to the child.
6	Start the steps of CPR if you know how. (See section on CPR.)

Remember: Children with diabetes who are not acting normally may have an injury or illness that is unrelated to diabetes. Be sure to check the child for other injuries and illnesses.

> ### FYI: Diabetic Emergency Supplies
>
> Children with diabetes often have emergency supplies with them in case of low blood sugar. Make sure any children with diabetes who are in your care have these supplies with them at all times.

If you are a child care worker or teacher, diabetic medications must be on hand and must be out of reach of the other children.

 Check your state regulations for additional details.

First Aid Action Plan for Diabetes and Low Blood Sugar

Caregivers and teachers must work together with the parents or guardians of a child with diabetes to help manage the child's diabetes. The best way to do this is with a first aid action plan for managing diabetes and low blood sugar. This plan includes information on

- What triggers low blood sugar
- How often to test blood sugar levels if you have been trained to do so
- What foods or drinks to give a child who shows signs of low blood sugar
- How to use a prescribed glucagon emergency kit (make sure the kit has not expired)
- What medical identification the child wears to be sure to receive proper treatment in an emergency.

Seizures

What You Will Learn

By the end of this section you should be able to

- Tell the signs of a seizure
- List the first aid actions for a person having a seizure

Some Causes of Seizures

A medical condition called epilepsy often causes seizures. But *not all* seizures are due to epilepsy. Seizures can also be caused by

- Head injury
- Low blood sugar
- Heat-related injury
- Poisons
- Fever

Signs of a Seizure

During some types of seizures, the child may

- Lose muscle control
- Fall to the ground
- Have jerking movements of the arms and legs and sometimes other parts of the body
- Stop responding

**Actions for
a Seizure**

Most seizures stop within a few minutes. Follow these steps if you suspect a child is having a seizure:

Step	Action
1	Protect the child from injury by • Moving furniture or other objects out of the child's way • Placing a pad or towel under the child's head
2	Phone or send someone to phone your emergency response number (or 911) if • This is the child's first seizure • You are unsure whether the child has had a seizure before • Your first aid action plan for this child says to do so
3	After the seizure, check to see if the child is breathing. If the child does not respond, start the steps of CPR if you know how.
4	If you do not suspect that the child has a head, neck, or spine injury, roll the child to her side.
5	Stay with the child until she starts responding.
6	If you have phoned your emergency response number (or 911), stay with the child until trained help arrives and takes over.

After a seizure it is not unusual for the child to be confused or to fall asleep.

Your day care center or school should have a first aid action plan for every child with a known seizure disorder. If a child has a seizure, send another adult for the plan.

Some children may wet or soil their pants during a seizure. If possible, try to protect the child's privacy during a seizure. Be prepared to cover the child's pants with a blanket until the child wakes and can change clothes.

> **Do Not**
> - *Do not* hold the child down.
> - *Do not* put anything in the child's mouth.
>
> The child may bite his tongue during a seizure. You can give first aid for that injury after the seizure stops.

Shock

**What You
Will Learn**

By the end of this section you should be able to

- List the signs of shock
- List the first aid actions for shock

What Is Shock?

Shock develops when there is not enough blood flowing to the cells of the body. In children shock is most often present if the child

- Has lost fluid, such as with vomiting or diarrhea
- Loses a lot of blood that you can see or that you can't see
- Has a bad allergic reaction

Signs of Shock

A child in shock may

- Feel weak, faint, or dizzy
- Have pale or grayish skin
- Act restless, agitated, or confused
- Be cold and clammy to the touch

Actions for Shock

Follow these steps when giving first aid to a child showing signs of shock:

Step	Action
1	Make sure the scene is safe for you and the child.
2	Phone or send someone to phone your emergency response number (or 911) and get the first aid kit.
3	Help the child lie on her back.
4	If there is no leg injury or pain, raise the child's legs just above the level of the child's heart (Figure 20).
5	Use pressure to stop bleeding that you can see. (See "Bleeding You Can See" on page 53.)
6	Cover the child to keep the child warm (you can use a Mylar blanket if there is one in the first aid kit).

Figure 20. If you suspect the child is in shock, raise the child's legs just above the level of the child's heart. Cover the child with a blanket.

Test Questions

Question	Your Notes
1. *True or false:* When giving abdominal thrusts to a child who is choking, you should put the thumb side of your fist slightly above her navel (belly button) and well below the breastbone. Circle your answer:　True　False	
2. *True or false:* If a 5-year-old child is eating and suddenly coughs and cannot breathe, talk, or make any sounds, you should tell the child you are going to help and give abdominal thrusts. Circle your answer:　True　False	
3. *True or false:* Signs of a bad allergic reaction include trouble breathing, swelling of the face and tongue, and fainting. Circle your answer:　True　False	
4. *True or false:* If a child with low blood sugar is responding and can sit up and swallow, you should give the child something that contains sugar to eat or drink. Circle your answer:　True　False	
5. *True or false:* If a child is having a seizure, you should try to put something in his mouth so he won't bite his tongue. Circle your answer:　True　False	
6. *True or false:* When a child is having a seizure, you should try to hold the child down to protect the child from injury. Circle your answer:　True　False	

Injury Emergencies

What You Will Learn

By the end of this section you should be able to

- List the first aid actions for bleeding that you can see
- Show how to stop bleeding

Bleeding You Can See

Bleeding is one of the most frightening emergencies. But many cuts are small and you can easily stop the bleeding. When a large blood vessel is cut or torn, the child can lose a large amount of blood within minutes. That's why you have to act fast.

Remember:

- Remain calm.
- You can stop most bleeding with pressure.
- Bleeding often looks a lot worse than it is.

Actions for Bleeding You Can See

Take the following actions to stop bleeding that you can see:

Step	Action
1	Make sure that the scene is safe for you and the child.
2	Send someone to get the first aid kit.
3	Wear personal protective equipment if appropriate.
4	Put firm pressure on the dressing (see the "FYI: Dressings" below) over the bleeding area with the flat part of your fingers or the palm of your hand (Figure 21).
5	If the bleeding does not stop, do not remove the dressing. Add a second dressing and press harder (Figure 22). If you remove the first dressing, it might pull off some blood clots and cause the wound to bleed more.
6	Check for signs of shock.
7	Phone or send someone to phone your emergency response number (or 911) if • There is a lot of bleeding • You cannot stop the bleeding • You see signs of shock • The injury is from a fall and you suspect a head, neck, or spine injury • You are not sure what to do

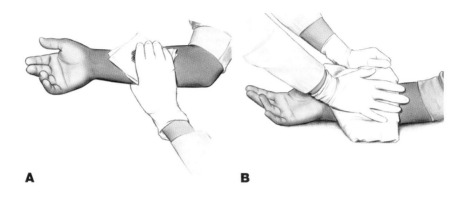

A   **B**

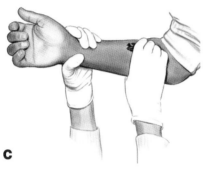

Figure 21. A dressing can be a gauze pad **(A)** or any other piece of cloth **(B)**. If you do not have a dressing, you may even use your gloved hand **(C)**.

C

FYI: Dressings

Use dressings to

- Stop bleeding with pressure
- Keep the wound clean

A dressing can be a gauze pad (see Figure 21A) or any other clean piece of cloth (see Figure 21B). Gauze pads come in different sizes. You should be able to find them in your first aid kit. Choose a size that covers the wound. Use sterile gauze pads on an open wound to lower the chance of infection. If you don't have a sterile dressing, use any clean cloth, such as a scarf or a shirt. You may even use your gloved hand (see Figure 21C).

Figure 22. If a dressing becomes soaked with blood, add more dressings and press harder.

Actions for Minor Cuts and Scrapes

You can stop bleeding with minor cuts and scrapes using pressure. Follow these steps for minor cuts and scrapes:

Step	Action
1	Make sure the scene is safe for you and the child.
2	Send someone to get the first aid kit.
3	Put on personal protective equipment if appropriate.
4	Wash the wound well with water and soap if available.
5	Stop the bleeding with pressure.
6	Apply a dressing or bandage to the wound.

FYI: Antibiotic Creams

Wounds heal better and with less infection if an antibiotic ointment or cream is used. Triple antibiotic ointment appears to be better than single antibiotic ointment or cream.

Apply antibiotic ointment or cream only if the child's wound is a small scrape or surface cut.

Actions for Major Cuts and Scrapes

Follow these steps if the cut or scrape is major and the child is bleeding a lot:

Step	Action
1	Make sure the scene is safe for you and the child.
2	Phone or send someone to phone your emergency response number (or 911) and get the first aid kit.
3	Put on personal protective equipment if appropriate.
4	Stop any bleeding you can see, using the skills you learned above.
5	Check for signs of shock.
6	Stay with the child until trained help arrives and takes over.

Special Areas of Bleeding You Can See

This section tells you how to give first aid for bleeding from the

- Nose
- Mouth
- Tooth

Bleeding From the Nose

With nosebleeds it can be hard to know how much bleeding there is because the child often swallows some of the blood. This may cause the child to vomit.

Actions for Bleeding From the Nose

Follow these steps when giving first aid to a child with a nosebleed:

Step	Action
1	Make sure the scene is safe for you and the child.
2	Send someone to get the first aid kit.
3	Put on personal protective equipment if appropriate.
4	Press both sides of the child's nostrils while the child sits and leans *forward* (Figure 23).
5	Place constant pressure on both sides of the nostrils for a few minutes until the bleeding stops.
6	If bleeding continues, press harder.
7	Phone or send someone to phone your emergency response number (or 911) if • You can't stop the bleeding in about 15 minutes • The bleeding is heavy, such as gushing blood • The child has trouble breathing

Figure 23. To stop a nosebleed, press both sides of the child's nostrils while the child sits and leans forward.

Do Not

• *Do not* ask the child to lean his head back.

• *Do not* use an icepack on the nose or forehead.

• *Do not* press on the bridge of the nose between the eyes (the upper bony part of the nose).

Bleeding From the Mouth

Like other bleeding you can see, you can usually stop bleeding from the mouth with pressure. But bleeding from the mouth can be serious if blood or broken teeth block the airway and cause breathing problems or if you can't reach the bleeding area.

Actions for Bleeding From the Mouth

Follow these steps when giving first aid to a child with bleeding from the mouth:

Step	Action
1	Make sure the scene is safe for you and the child.
2	Send someone to get the first aid kit.
3	Put on personal protective equipment if appropriate.
4	If the bleeding is from the tongue, lip, or cheek or another area you can easily reach, press the bleeding area with a sterile gauze or clean cloth (Figure 24).
5	If bleeding is deep in the mouth and you can't reach it easily, roll the child to his side.
6	Check for signs of shock.
7	Watch the child's breathing. Be ready to start the steps of CPR if needed and if you know how (see the section on CPR).
8	Phone or send someone to phone your emergency response number (or 911) if • You can't stop the bleeding • The child has trouble breathing

Figure 24. If the bleeding is from the tongue, lip, or cheek, press the bleeding area with a sterile gauze or clean cloth.

Tooth Injuries

Children with a mouth injury may have broken, loose, or knocked-out teeth. This can be a choking hazard, especially for young children.

Actions for Tooth Injuries

Follow these steps when giving first aid to a child with a tooth injury:

Step	Action
1	Make sure the scene is safe for you and the child.
2	Send someone to get the first aid kit.
3	Put on personal protective equipment if appropriate.
4	Check the child's mouth for any missing teeth, loose teeth, or parts of teeth.
5	If a tooth is loose, have the child bite down on a piece of gauze to keep the tooth in place and call the child's parent/guardian or dentist.
6	If a tooth is chipped, gently clean the injured area and call the child's parent/guardian or dentist.
7	If the child has lost a permanent tooth, rinse the tooth in water, put the tooth in a cup of milk, and immediately take the child and tooth to a dentist or emergency department.
8	Apply pressure with gauze to stop any bleeding at the tooth socket.
9	Tell the child's parent/guardian to talk with a dentist if a child's tooth changes color after an injury.

Do Not

- *Do not* hold the tooth by the root. Hold the tooth by only the crown (the part of the tooth that does not go into the gums).
- *Do not* try to reinsert the tooth.

Bleeding You Can't See

What You Will Learn

By the end of this section you should be able to

- Tell when you should suspect bleeding inside the body
- List the first aid actions for bleeding you can't see

Bleeding You Can't See

A strong blow to the chest or abdomen or a fall can cause injury and bleeding inside the body. You may not see signs of this bleeding on the outside of the body at all, or you may see a bruise on the skin over the injured part of the body. An injury inside the body may be minor or severe.

When to Suspect Bleeding You Can't See

Suspect bleeding inside the body if a child has

- An injury from a car crash, a pedestrian injury, or a fall from a height
- An injury to the abdomen or chest (including bruises such as seat belt marks)
- Sports injuries such as running into other children hard or being hit with a ball or bat
- Pain in the chest or abdomen after an injury
- Shortness of breath after an injury
- Coughed-up or vomited blood after an injury
- Signs of shock without bleeding that you can see

Actions for Bleeding You Can't See

Follow these steps when giving first aid to a child who may have bleeding you can't see:

Step	Action
1	Make sure the scene is safe for you and the child.
2	Phone or send someone to phone your emergency response number (or 911) and get the first aid kit and AED if available.
3	Gently try to keep the child still and lying down.
4	Check for signs of shock.
5	If the child stops responding, start the steps of CPR (see the section on CPR).

Wounds

What You Will Learn

By the end of this section you should be able to

- Tell what to do with splinters
- Tell what to do with injuries from puncturing objects
- List the first aid steps for an amputated part of the body

Splinters

Splinters are small pieces of wood or metal that stick under the skin.

If your regulatory agency allows it, you can try to remove a splinter.

Actions for Splinters

Follow these steps when giving first aid to a child with a splinter:

Step	Action
1	Make sure the scene is safe for you and the child.
2	Get the first aid kit.
3	Try using sticky tape to remove a splinter. Put the tape over the splinter and pull the tape off. The splinter may stick to the tape and come out.
4	If tape doesn't work, wash your hands well with soap and water.
5	Hold the end of the splinter with clean tweezers and gently pull it out.
6	After you have removed the splinter, clean the child's wound with water and soap if available.
7	The child may need medical care if the splinter • Is large • Is deeply embedded in the skin • Is difficult to remove • Is in the eye • Broke off, possibly leaving part of it in the wound • Becomes infected

---

Do Not

- *Do not* try to remove a splinter in the eye. See the section on eye injuries.
- *Do not* wet or soak the splinter because it will be harder to remove in one piece.
- *Do not* try to hunt around for the splinter with a needle or other sharp object.

Injuries From Puncturing Objects

An object such as a knife or sharp stick can cause a penetrating injury or an injury that punctures the skin. It is important not to remove the object. Leave it in place until a healthcare provider can treat the injury.

Actions for Injuries From Puncturing Objects

Follow these steps when giving first aid to a child with an injury from a puncturing object:

Step	Action
1	Make sure the scene is safe for you and the child.
2	Phone or send someone to phone your emergency response number (or 911) and get the first aid kit.
3	Put on personal protective equipment if appropriate.
4	Stop any bleeding you can see.
5	Try to keep the child from moving.
6	Check for signs of shock.

Do Not

If a person is injured and a sharp object, such as a nail or a knife, remains partly stuck in the body, *do not* take it out. Taking it out may cause more damage.

Amputations

If a part of the body, such as a finger, toe, hand, or foot, is cut off (amputated), you should save the body part because doctors may be able to reattach it. You can preserve a detached body part at room temperature, but it will be in better condition to be reattached if you keep it cool.

Actions for Amputation

Follow these steps when giving first aid to a child with an amputation:

Step	Action
1	Make sure the scene is safe for you and the child.
2	Phone or send someone to phone your emergency response number (or 911) and get the first aid kit.
3	Put on personal protective equipment if appropriate.
4	Stop the bleeding from the injured area with pressure. You will have to press for a long time with very firm pressure to stop the bleeding.
5	Look for signs of shock and give first aid as needed.
6	If you find the amputated part, refer to "Protecting an Amputated Part."
7	Stay with the child until trained help arrives and takes over.

Protecting an Amputated Part

Follow these steps to protect an amputated part:

Step	Action
1	Rinse the amputated part with clean water (Figure 25A).
2	Cover or wrap the amputated part with a clean dressing.
3	If it will fit, place the amputated part in a watertight plastic bag (Figure 25B).
4	Place that bag in another container with ice or ice and water; label it with the child's name, date, and time (Figure 25C).
5	Make sure it is sent to the hospital with the child.

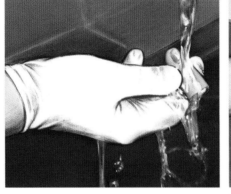

A

B

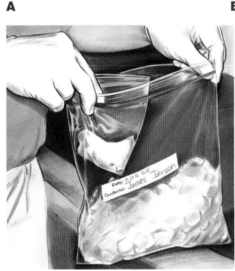

C

Figure 25. A, Rinse the amputated part with clean water. Then cover or wrap it with a clean dressing. **B**, If it will fit, place it in a watertight plastic bag. **C**, Place that bag in another container with ice or ice and water, label it with the child's name, date, and time, and make sure to send it to the hospital with the child.

Do Not

Never place the amputated body part directly on ice or in water because the ice or water may damage it.

What You Will Learn

By the end of this section you should be able to

- List signs of head, neck, and spine injury
- List first aid actions for a child with a possible head, neck, and spine injury

When to Suspect a Head Injury

You should suspect that the child has a head injury if the child

- Fell from a height
- Was hit in the head
- Was injured while diving
- Was electrocuted
- Was involved in a car crash
- Was riding a bicycle or motorbike, was involved in a crash, and has no helmet or a broken helmet

> **FYI: Falling From a Height**
>
> If a child falls from a height greater than the child's height, you should suspect a head, neck, or spine injury.

Important: Shaken Baby Syndrome

The brain of an infant is very sensitive to motion. Shaking a baby can seriously injure the baby. It might even kill the baby. Be sure to handle a baby carefully to protect him or her from injury.

If you suspect that a baby has been shaken, you must report it to your state's Child Protective Services. For more information, see the section "Suspected Abuse" on page 96.

Signs of Head Injury

You should suspect that a child has a head injury if after an injury the child

- Does not respond or only moves or moans and groans
- Is sleepy or confused
- Vomits
- Complains of a headache
- Has trouble seeing
- Has trouble walking or moving any part of the body
- Has a seizure

Neck and Spine Injuries

The bones of the spine protect the spinal cord. The spinal cord carries messages between the brain and the body.

If these bones are broken, the spinal cord may be injured. The child may not be able to move his legs or arms and may lose feeling in parts of the body. Some people call this a "broken back."

> **Important**
>
> *You may cause further injury to the spinal cord if you bend, twist, or turn the child's head or neck. When you give first aid to a child with a possible spine injury, you must not bend, twist, or turn the head or neck!*

When to Suspect a Neck or Spine Injury

You should suspect that the child's neck or spine may be injured if a child

- Has an injury to the upper part of the body, especially the head, back, or chest
- Was injured by a falling object or a forceful blow to the head or chest
- Was in a motor vehicle crash (in the vehicle or as a pedestrian)
- Fell from a height
- Was injured while under the influence of drugs or alcohol (for older children)
- Had an injury that caused the child to stop responding
- Is not fully alert
- Complains of neck or back pain, tingling in the arms or legs, or weakness
- Is injured while diving

Actions for Head, Neck, and Spine Injuries

Follow these steps when giving first aid to a child with a possible head, neck, or spine injury:

Step	Action
1	Make sure the scene is safe for you and the child.
2	Phone or send someone to phone your emergency response number (or 911) and get the first aid kit.
3	Hold the head and neck so that they do not move, bend, or twist (Figure 26A).
4	Only turn or move the child if • The child is in danger • You need to do so to check breathing or open the child's airway • The child is vomiting
5	If the child does not respond, start the steps of CPR as needed if you know how.
6	If you must turn the child, be sure to roll the child while you support the child's head, neck, and body in a straight line so that they do not twist, bend, or turn in any direction (Figure 26B). This requires 2 rescuers.
7	If the child responds and is vomiting, roll the child onto her side.

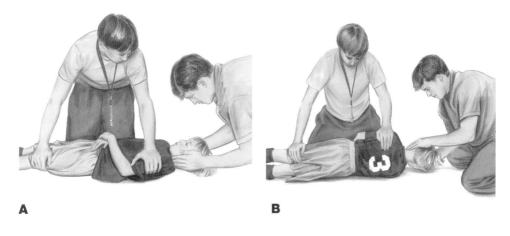

A B

Figure 26. Support the child's head, neck, and upper body **(A)** so that the head and neck stay in line and do not twist, bend, or turn in any direction if you must roll the child **(B)**.

Broken Bones, Sprains, and Bruises

What You Will Learn

By the end of this section you should be able to list the first aid actions for broken bones, sprains, and bruises.

Broken Bones, Sprains, and Bruises

Broken bones, sprains, and bruises are common in children. Without an x-ray it may be impossible to tell whether a bone is broken. But you will perform the same actions even if you don't know whether the bone is actually broken.

Joint Sprains

Joint sprains result from a twisting injury. The twisting injury causes tears in muscles and other structures around the joint. The tears cause pain. They may cause pain, swelling, and a blue color over the joint. Ice and rest decrease the amount of joint pain and swelling and help the joint to heal faster.

Bruises

A child may get a bruise if he is hit or runs into a hard object. Bruises happen when blood collects under the skin. They can appear as red or black-and-blue spots. You can reduce swelling by applying ice to the bruised area.

Actions for Broken Bones and Sprains

Follow these steps when giving first aid to a child with a possible broken bone or sprain:

Step	Action
1	Make sure the scene is safe for you and the child.
2	Send someone to get the first aid kit. If you are alone, go get the first aid kit.
3	Put on personal protective equipment if appropriate.
4	Check for signs of shock.
5	Don't try to straighten or move any injured part that is bent, deformed, or possibly broken (such as an arm, a leg, or a finger).
6	Cover any open wound with a clean dressing.
7	Put a plastic bag filled with ice on the injured area with a towel between the ice bag and the skin for up to 20 minutes (Figure 27).
8	Raise the injured body part if doing so does not cause the child more pain.
9	Phone or send someone to phone your emergency response number (or 911) if • There is a large open wound • The injured part is abnormally bent • You're not sure what to do
10	If it is painful, the child should avoid using an injured body part until checked by a healthcare provider.

FYI: If Ice Is Not Available

You can use a bag of frozen vegetables if ice is not available. You may use a cold pack, but it is not as cold and may not work as well as ice.

Figure 27. Put a plastic bag filled with ice on the bruise with a towel between the ice bag and the skin.

Splinting

A splint keeps an injured body part from moving. In general, healthcare providers apply splints.

At times, however, you may need to splint a child's arm or leg. For example, if you are hiking in the wilderness and are far from healthcare providers, you may need to splint a child's injured arm or leg until you reach help.

Actions for Splinting

Follow these steps to splint a child's injured body part:

Step	Action
1	Make sure the scene is safe for you and the child.
2	For the splint, use something that will keep the arm or leg from moving from the position in which you found it. This may be a rolled up towel or magazine or a piece of wood (Figure 28).
3	The splint should ideally extend beyond the injured area and support the joints above and below the injury (Figure 28). For example, if the forearm is injured, the splint should extend from above the elbow to below the wrist.
4	Tie the splint to the injured body part so that it supports the injured area. Use tape, gauze, or cloth to secure it. You should be able to put a few fingers between the splint and the injured body part. Do not tie the splint too tightly. This might cause further pain.
5	Make sure the child is checked by a healthcare provider.

Figure 28. Use stiff material, such as a rolled up magazine, to splint injured body parts.

Self-splinting

To splint an arm, have the child place his hand across his chest or stomach and hold it in place with the other hand. This is "self-splinting." It helps the arm stay still until you have help from healthcare providers.

Do Not

- *Do not* straighten or move any injured part that is bent or deformed.
- *Do not* move a broken bone that has come through the skin. Instead, cover the wound with a clean dressing, and splint as needed.

Overview

Burns are injuries caused by contact with heat, electricity, or chemicals.

What You Will Learn

By the end of this section you should be able to

- List the first aid actions for burns
- List the first aid actions for a victim of electrocution

Actions for Small Burns

Follow these steps to give first aid to a child with a small burn:

Step	Action
1	Make sure the scene is safe for you and the child.
2	Send someone to get the first aid kit. If you are alone, go get the first aid kit.
3	If the burn area is small, cool it immediately with cold, but not ice cold, water (Figure 29).
4	You may cover the burn with a dry, nonstick sterile or clean dressing.
5	Phone or send someone to phone your emergency response number (or 911) if • There is a fire • The child has a large burn • You are not sure what to do
6	Contact the child's parent/guardian and the child's healthcare provider for any burn.

Figure 29. If the burn area is small, cool it immediately with cold, but not ice cold, water.

**Actions for
Large Burns**

Follow these steps to give first aid to a child with a large burn:

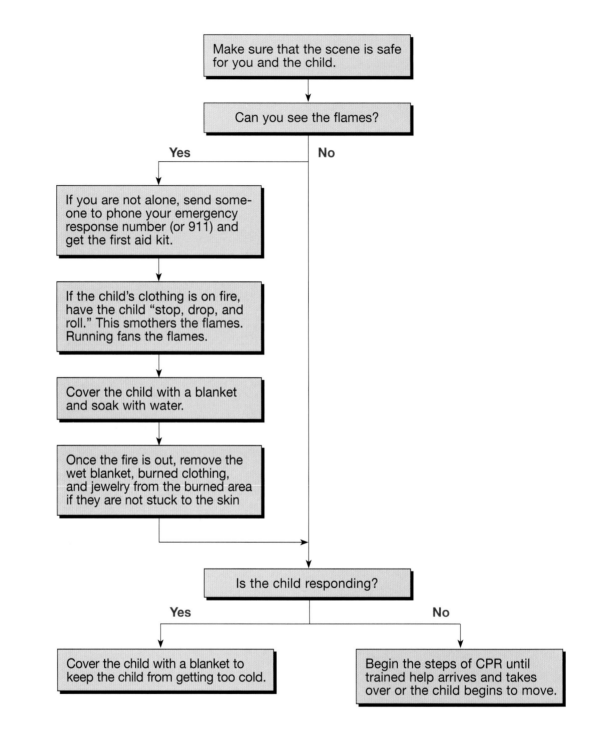

Make sure that the scene is safe for you and the child.

↓

Can you see the flames?

Yes ← | → No

Yes:

If you are not alone, send someone to phone your emergency response number (or 911) and get the first aid kit.

↓

If the child's clothing is on fire, have the child "stop, drop, and roll." This smothers the flames. Running fans the flames.

↓

Cover the child with a blanket and soak with water.

↓

Once the fire is out, remove the wet blanket, burned clothing, and jewelry from the burned area if they are not stuck to the skin

↓

Is the child responding?

Yes ← | → No

Yes: Cover the child with a blanket to keep the child from getting too cold.

No: Begin the steps of CPR until trained help arrives and takes over or the child begins to move.

Contact the child's parent/guardian and healthcare provider for any burn.

FYI: Sunburns

Sunburns are a common type of burn, especially in children. They are typically mild but can be painful and cause blisters.

You can prevent sunburn by following these suggestions:

- Keep infants less than 6 months of age out of direct sunlight.
- For children older than 6 months of age, use sunscreen made for children.
- Put sunscreen on children before they go outside.
- Choose a water-resistant or waterproof sunscreen. Reapply waterproof sunscreen every 2 hours, especially if children are playing in the water.
- Try to stay out of the sun during the hottest part of the day (10 AM to 4 PM).

Causes of Electrocution and Electrical Injury

Electricity occurs naturally in the form of lightning or from man-made sources like an electrical current from an outlet or electrical wire. Electricity can cause burns on the skin and injure organs inside the body.

If electricity enters the body, it can cause severe damage. It can even cause the child to stop breathing, or it can cause an abnormal heart rhythm that can be deadly. You may see marks or wounds where the electricity has entered and left the body. These marks may seem very small, but *you can't tell from the outside of the body how much damage there is inside the body!*

FYI: Toddlers and Electrical Outlets

A curious toddler may try to stick something into an uncovered electrical outlet. Cover electrical outlets with protective covers to help prevent this type of injury.

Actions for Electrical Injury

Follow these steps to give first aid to a child with an electrical injury:

Step	Action
1	Make sure the scene is safe for you and the child. Do not touch the child as long as the child is in contact with the power source. (See "FYI: Electrocution and Power Supplies" below.)
2	Phone or send someone to phone your emergency response number (or 911) and get an AED if one is available. (See section on AED.)
3	When it is safe to touch the child, check for a response. If the child does not respond or stops responding, start the steps of CPR and use the AED if available. (See the sections on CPR and AED.)
4	Check for signs of shock.
5	A healthcare provider should check all children who have an electrical injury.

FYI: Electrocution and Power Supplies

Do not touch the child as long as the child is in contact with the power source while the power is on. Electricity can travel from the source through the child to you. It's best to turn off the main power switch (usually located near the fuse box).

If the electrocution is caused by *high voltage,* such as a fallen power line, immediately notify the proper authorities (phone your emergency response number or 911). Remember that if the voltage is high enough, it can travel through *everything* that touches the power line or source (even a wooden stick) and can hurt you. *Don't enter the area around the child.* Don't try to pull away wires or other materials until the power has been turned off.

Do Not
- *Do not* put ointment on a burn unless a healthcare provider tells you to do so.
- *Do not* put any medicine or household product on a burn unless a healthcare provider tells you to do so.
- *Do not* put anything on the burn except a dry dressing. Do not apply butter or oil to a burn.
- *Do not* break any blisters that form after the burn.

Question	Your Notes
1. *True or false:* To help stop bleeding that you can see, put firm pressure on a dressing or bandage over the bleeding area. Circle your answer: True False	
2. *True or false:* To care for a child with a nose-bleed, press both sides of the child's nostrils and have the child lie down. Circle your answer: True False	
3. *Fill in the blank with the correct word or words.* If a child is showing signs of shock, you should help the child lie on his back and raise his _____ just above the level of the child's heart.	
4. *True or false:* You should use sticky tape or tweezers to try to remove a splinter. Circle your answer: True False	
5. *True or false:* If a large stick or a knife has been pushed into the child's body, you should remove it as quickly as possible. Circle your answer: True False	
6. *True or false:* If a child falls down and then becomes sleepy or confused or vomits or complains of a head-ache, the child may have a head injury. Circle your answer: True False	
7. True or false: As soon as a child twists his ankle, apply a heating pad or heat pack over the injured area for 20 minutes to help reduce swelling. Circle your answer: *True False*	
8. True or false: To give first aid for a small burn on the arm, cool the burn with cold but not ice cold water. Circle your answer: *True False*	

Environmental Emergencies

Bites and Stings

What You Will Learn

By the end of this section you should be able to list the first aid actions for bites and stings.

Animal and Human Bites

Young, preschool-aged children sometimes bite each other. Some young children will bite others to show their feelings. Most children stop biting when they grow older.

Animal bites are less common and can often be prevented. Unfortunately when they do occur, animal bites can be serious.

Although many bites are minor, some may break the skin. Both animal and human mouths have many germs. When a bite breaks the skin, the wound can bleed and may become infected from the germs in the child's or animal's mouth. Bites that do not break the skin usually are not serious.

Actions for Animal and Human Bites

Follow these steps to give first aid to a child with an animal or human bite:

Step	Action
1	Make sure the scene is safe for you and the child.
2	Stay away from any animal that is acting strangely. An animal with rabies can bite again. (See "Important: Rabies" below.)
3	For animal bites, phone or send someone to phone your emergency response number (or 911) and get the first aid kit.
4	Put on personal protective equipment if appropriate.
5	Clean the child's wound with running water (and soap if available).
6	Stop any bleeding with pressure.
7	Report all animal bites to the police or an animal control officer. Describe • The animal • How the bite happened • The location of the animal when last seen
8	For all bites, call the parent/guardian or healthcare provider or both. For bites that break the skin, call the child's healthcare provider because the child might need shots or other medicine to treat the bite.
9	If there is a bruise or swelling, place an ice bag wrapped in a towel on the bite for up to 20 minutes.

Important: Stopping Severe Bleeding

If there is severe bleeding that will not stop, apply pressure and treat the injury like a major cut or scrape.

Important: Rabies

Assume that an animal has rabies if

- The animal attacks without being provoked
- The animal behaves in an unusual manner (for example, if a usually friendly dog attacks)
- The animal is a skunk, raccoon, fox, bat, or other wild animal
- You are not sure

Insect, Bee, and Spider Bites and Stings

Usually insect, bee, and spider bites and stings cause only mild pain, itching, and swelling at the bite.

Some insect bites can be serious and even fatal if

- The child has a bad allergic reaction to the bite or sting
- Poison (venom) is injected into the child (for example, a black widow spider or brown recluse spider)

Actions for Insect, Bee, and Spider Bites and Stings

Follow these steps to give first aid to a child with an insect, bee, or spider bite or sting:

Step	Action
1	Make sure the scene is safe for you and the child.
2	Phone or send someone to phone your emergency response number (or 911) and get the first aid kit if • The child has signs of a bad allergic reaction • The child tells you that he has a bad allergic reaction to insect bites or stings
3	If a bee stung the child • Look for the stinger. Bees are the only insects that may leave their stingers behind. • Scrape away the stinger and venom sac using something with a dull edge such as a credit card.
4	Wash the bite or sting area with running water (and soap if possible).
5	Put an ice bag wrapped in a towel or cloth over the bite or sting area to help reduce swelling.
6	Watch the child for at least 30 minutes for signs of a bad allergic reaction (see below).

Do Not

Do not pull the stinger out with tweezers or your fingers. Squeezing the venom sac can release more poison (venom).

Signs of a Bad Allergic Reaction

Some children can have a bad allergic reaction to insect bites, especially to bee stings. People who have bad allergic reactions to insect bites often have an epinephrine pen and know how to use it. They often wear medical identification jewelry. If a child has a bad allergy to insect bites, you must have a first aid action plan, you must know where the child's epinephrine pen is located, and you must know how to use it.

Signs of a bad allergic reaction are

- Trouble breathing
- Swelling of the tongue and face
- Fainting

Actions for a Bad Allergic Reaction

Follow these steps to give first aid to a child with a bad allergic reaction:

Step	Action
1	Phone or send someone to phone your emergency response number (or 911) and get the first aid kit.
2	Help the child get the epinephrine pen and use it if your state and workplace allow you to.
3	If the child stops responding, start the steps of CPR if you know how. (See the section on CPR.)

Temperature-Related Emergencies

What You Will Learn

By the end of this section you should be able to

- List the signs of a heat-related emergency
- List the first aid actions for a heat-related emergency
- List the signs of a cold-related emergency
- List the first aid actions for a cold-related emergency

Heat-Related Emergencies

Children exposed to heat can experience heat-related emergencies. To avoid heat-related emergencies

- Do not leave children alone in a hot, parked car.
- Dress children appropriately for the weather.
- Make sure children drink plenty of fluids during hot weather.

Signs and Actions for Heat-Related Emergencies

Heat-related emergencies can range from mild to life-threatening. You must recognize and give first aid for heat-related emergencies early because a child with mild signs can get worse quickly and develop potentially life-threatening problems, such as heatstroke. Children are especially sensitive to extreme temperatures.

Many of the signs of a heat-related emergency are similar to those of the flu.

The following table shows signs and actions for heat-related emergencies and heat stroke:

Signs	Actions
Heat-Related Emergency • Muscle cramps • Sweating • Headache • Nausea • Weakness • Dizziness	1. Move the child to a cool or shady area. 2. Loosen or remove tight clothing from the child. 3. Encourage the child to drink water if the child can sit up and swallow. 4. Sponge or spray the child with cool *(not ice cold)* water and fan the child. 5. Phone or send someone to phone your emergency response number (or 911) immediately if there are any signs of heat-stroke. Continue to cool the child until the child's behavior is normal again or trained help arrives and takes over. 6. If the child stops responding or does not get better, phone your emergency response number (or 911) and start the steps of CPR if you know how (see the section on CPR).
Heatstroke • Confusion or strange behavior • Vomiting • Inability to drink • Red, hot, and dry skin (the child may stop sweating) • Shallow breathing, seizures, or no response	1. Phone or send someone to phone your emergency response number (or 911). 2. Move the child to a cool or shady area. 3. Loosen or remove tight clothing. 4. Sponge or spray the child with cool *(not ice cold)* water and fan the child. Continue to cool the child until the child's behavior is normal again or trained help arrives and takes over. 5. If the child stops responding, start the steps of CPR if you know how (see the section on CPR).

Important

Remember that children are very sensitive to extreme heat. Symptoms of heat-related emergencies often get worse if left untreated. Mild heat-related signs are a warning that the child may get worse unless you take action!

Do Not

- *Do not* wait to begin cooling the child until trained help arrives and takes over. Every minute counts!
- *Do not* continue cooling the child once the child's behavior is normal again. Unnecessary cooling could lead to low body temperature (hypothermia).
- *Do not* put rubbing alcohol or anything other than water onto the child's skin.
- *Do not* give the child anything to drink or eat if the child cannot swallow or is vomiting, confused, has had a seizure, or is not responding.

Cold-Related Emergencies

Cold-related emergencies may involve only part of the body or the whole body. A cold injury to part of the body is called frostbite. Cold injury to the whole body is called low body temperature, or hypothermia.

To prevent cold-related emergencies

■ Make sure children wear appropriate clothing in cold weather.
■ Do not allow small children to stay outside in very cold weather without watching them closely. Make sure they can handle the cold and are keeping warm.

Frostbite

Frostbite affects parts of the body that are exposed to the cold, such as the fingers, toes, nose, and ears. Frostbite typically occurs outside in cold weather. But it can also occur inside when people without gloves handle extremely cold materials.

Signs of Frostbite

■ The skin over the frostbitten area is white, waxy, or grayish-yellow.
■ The frostbitten area is cold and numb.
■ The frostbitten area is hard, and the skin doesn't move when you push it.

Actions for Frostbite

Follow these steps for frostbite

Step	Action
1	Move the victim to a warm place.
2	Phone or send someone to phone your company's emergency response number (or 911) and get the first aid kit.
3	Remove tight clothing, rings, or bracelets from the frostbitten part.
4	Remove any wet clothing.
5	Do not try to thaw the frozen part if you are close to a medical facility or if you think there may be a chance of refreezing.

> **Do Not**
> - *Do not* rub or massage the frostbite.
> - *Do not* use a heating pad, stove, or fire to rewarm a frostbite.
> - *Do not thaw the frozen part if there is any chance of refreezing or if you are close to a medical facility.*

Low Body Temperature (Hypothermia)

Hypothermia occurs when body temperature falls. Hypothermia is a serious condition that can cause death. A child can develop hypothermia even when the temperature is above freezing. Infants can easily develop hypothermia.

Signs of Low Body Temperature

Signs of low body temperature include the following:

- The child's skin is cool to the touch.
- Shivering (only when the child's body temperature falls a small amount but not when the body temperature is very low).
- The child may become confused, have a change in personality, or may be unconcerned about her condition.
- Muscles become stiff and rigid, and the skin gets ice cold and blue.

As the child's body temperature continues to drop

- The child stops responding
- The child's breathing slows
- It may be hard to tell whether the child is breathing
- The child may appear to be dead

Actions for Low Body Temperature

Follow these steps for low body temperature:

Step	Action
1	Get the child out of the cold.
2	Remove wet clothing and pat the child dry. Put dry clothes on the child if available and cover with a blanket.
3	Phone or send someone to phone your emergency response number (or 911) and get the first aid kit and AED if available.
4	Put blankets or towels under and around the child, and cover the child's head but not the face.
5	If the child stops responding, start the steps of CPR (see the section on CPR).

FYI: Shivering

- Shivering protects the body by producing heat.
- Shivering stops when the body becomes very cold.

FYI: Rewarming the Child

If you are far from medical care, you can start to rewarm a child. Place the child near a heat source and place containers of warm, but not hot, water in contact with the skin. It is important to get the child to medical care as soon as possible.

Poison Emergencies

Overview

According to the American Association of Poison Control Centers, a poison is anything someone swallows, breathes, or gets in the eyes or on the skin that causes sickness or death if it gets into or on the body. Many products can poison people. This section will not deal with specific poisons. Instead it will cover general principles of first aid for a child exposed to a poison.

What You Will Learn

By the end of this section you should be able to tell the steps for giving first aid for poisoning.

Preventing Poisoning

To prevent poisonings, keep these items out of children's reach:

- All medicine, including vitamins
- Mouthwash
- Cleaning supplies
- Chemicals

Poison Control Center Contact Information

The poison control center can tell you the latest method to treat poisonings. The number below will connect you with your nearest poison control center. In many places the poison control hotline can also link the caller directly to the local emergency ambulance dispatch and the nearest hospital's emergency department.

The US National Poison Control Center phone number is 800-222-1222. Keep this number close to your phone and in your first aid kit.

Actions for Poisoning Emergencies

If you think a child may have touched, swallowed, or inhaled a poison

Step	Action
1	Make sure the scene is safe before you approach the child. Look out for spilled or leaking bottles or boxes. • If there is a chemical spill or the child is in an unsafe area, try to move the child to an area with fresh air if you can do so safely. • Ask everyone to move away from the area.
2	If the child does not respond, send someone to phone your emergency response number (or 911). You stay with the child and start the steps of CPR if you know how. Whenever possible, you should always try to use a mask when giving breaths. This is especially important if the poison is on the child's lips or mouth.
3	If the child does respond, phone the poison control center. Tell the poison control center the name of the poison if possible.
4	Remove the poison from the child's skin and clothing if you can do so safely. • Help the child take off contaminated clothing and jewelry. • Brush off any dry powder or solid substances from the child's skin with your gloved hand (Figure 30). • Run water over the skin, eyes, and other contaminated areas of the child's body for at least 20 minutes or until trained help arrives and takes over (Figure 31). Ask the child to blink as much as possible while rinsing his eyes.

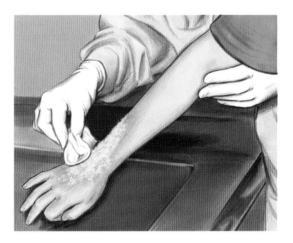

Figure 30. Brush off any dry powder or solid substances from the child's skin with your gloved hand.

Important: Washing the Affected Area

Remember that it is very important to wash the poison off the child using lots of water as soon as possible.

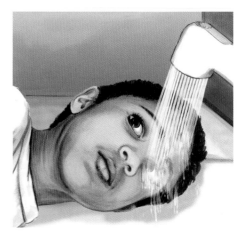

Figure 31. Help the child wash his eyes and face under a sink or an eye wash station.

Important: Poison in an Eye

If only one eye is affected, make sure the eye with the poison in it is the lower eye as you rinse the eyes. Make sure you do not rinse the poison into the unaffected eye.

General Groups of Poisons

The following table lists general groups of poisons and other possibly dangerous substances. These poisons can enter the body by swallowing, breathing, or touching. This information is for reference only. It does not include all possible classifications or all poisonous substances. The first aid rescuer is not expected to memorize these.

Classification	Examples of Poisons
Plants	Dieffenbachia Foxglove Poison ivy Poison sumac Poison oak Philodendron
Gases	Carbon monoxide Propane Methane and natural gas
Corrosives/acids	Pool cleaner Chlorine Ammonia
Hydrocarbons	Enamel paint Diesel fuel or gasoline Lighter fluid Turpentine

Classification	Examples of Poisons
Household products	Drain cleaners
	Oven cleaners
	Toilet bowl cleaners
	Disinfectants
	Laundry detergents
	Bleach
	Pesticides and insecticides
	Alcoholic beverages
	Rubbing alcohol
	Furniture polish
	Gasoline, kerosene
	Antifreeze
	Windshield cleaner
Personal care products	Mouthwash
	Perfume and cologne
	Nail polish and polish remover
Medicines/vitamins	Nonprescription medicines, including aspirin, acetaminophen, ibuprofen, antacids, laxatives, vitamins
	Prescription medicines
Other chemicals	Glues and adhesives

Do Not

- *Do not* give the child anything by mouth unless you have been told to do so by trained help or the poison control center. This includes water, milk, syrup of ipecac, and activated charcoal.
- *Do not* rely on only the first aid instructions on the label of the bottle, can, or box.
- *Do not* apply any ointments or lotions to the skin.

FYI: Calling the Poison Control Center

When you phone the poison control center, try to have the following information ready:

- What is the name of the poison? Can you describe it if you cannot name it?
- How much poison did the child touch, breathe, or swallow?
- About how old is the child? What is the child's approximate weight?
- When did the poisoning happen?
- How is the child feeling or acting now?

Drownings

What You Will Learn

By the end of this section you should be able to list the first aid actions for drowning.

Drowning

Drowning is the third most common accidental cause of death in children under 15 years of age. Children are very attracted to water. Young children can drown in very shallow water or even in the bathtub.

FYI: Water Safety

Do not leave a child alone around any water. The head of an infant or a small child is very heavy compared with the rest of his body. Infants and small children can lean and fall into a bucket, toilet, or small container and be unable to lift their head out of the water.

Swimming pools, creeks, fountains, lakes, and rivers are very interesting to most children. It is important to closely watch all children near pools or other bodies of water. Any infant or child can drown, even if the child knows how to swim. Always stay within reach of a child near a body of water.

Actions for Drowning

Follow these steps for drowning:

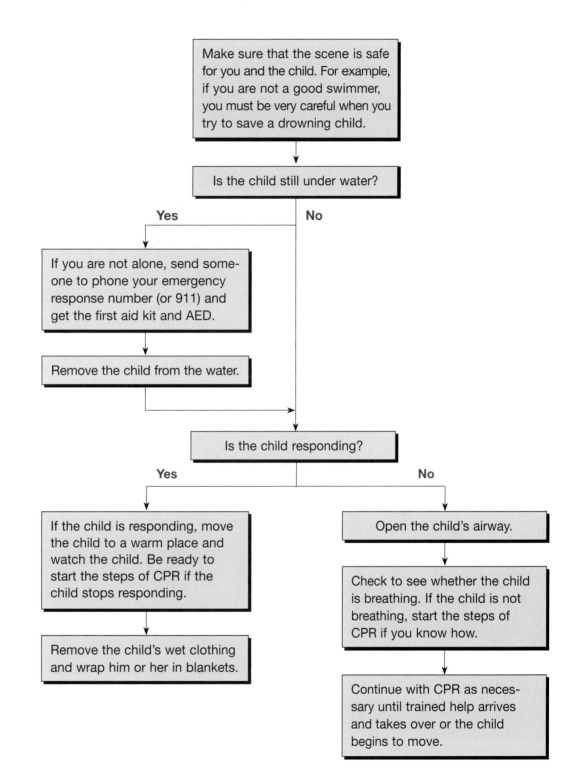

Make sure that the scene is safe for you and the child. For example, if you are not a good swimmer, you must be very careful when you try to save a drowning child.

↓

Is the child still under water?

Yes — **No**

If you are not alone, send someone to phone your emergency response number (or 911) and get the first aid kit and AED.

↓

Remove the child from the water.

Is the child responding?

Yes — **No**

If the child is responding, move the child to a warm place and watch the child. Be ready to start the steps of CPR if the child stops responding.

↓

Remove the child's wet clothing and wrap him or her in blankets.

Open the child's airway.

↓

Check to see whether the child is breathing. If the child is not breathing, start the steps of CPR if you know how.

↓

Continue with CPR as necessary until trained help arrives and takes over or the child begins to move.

FYI: Drowning in Cold Water

Children who drown in cold water may appear dead with stiff muscles, no breathing, and cold blue skin. Start the steps of CPR right away and continue until trained help arrives and takes over.

Test Questions

Questions	Your Notes
1. *True or false:* You should watch a child for at least 30 minutes after the child has been bit by an insect, bee, or spider because the child may develop signs of a bad allergic reaction. Circle your answer:　　True　　False	
2. *True or false:* When a child is having a heat-related emergency, you should move the child to a cool place and sponge or spray the child with cool water and fan the child. Circle your answer:　　True　　False	
3. *True or false:* A child with heatstroke will have red, hot, and dry skin and may be confused or have strange behavior. Circle your answer:　　True　　False	
4. *True or false:* A child with low body temperature will have cool skin and may shiver or become confused. Circle your answer:　　True　　False	
5. *True or false:* If you think a child has swallowed a poison, you should help the child drink several glasses of water or milk before phoning poison control. Circle your answer:　　True　　False	
6. *True or false:* Young children can drown in very shallow water or even in the bathtub. Circle your answer:　　True　　False	

Optional Topics

Eye Injuries

What You Will Learn

By the end of this section you should be able to list first aid actions for a child with an eye injury.

Signs of Eye Injuries

Eye injuries may happen with a

- Direct hit or punch in the eye or to the side of the head
- Ball or other object that directly hits the eye
- High-speed object that strikes the eye, like a BB gun pellet
- Stick or other sharp object that punctures the eye
- Small object in the eye, such as a piece of dirt, an eyelash, a piece of sand, or pollen
- Chemical that splashes in the eye

Signs of eye injury include

- Pain
- Trouble seeing
- Bruising
- Bleeding
- Redness, swelling

Actions for Eye Injuries

Follow these steps for eye injuries:

Step	Action
1	Make sure the scene is safe for you and the child.
2	Send someone to get the first aid kit. If you are alone, go get the first aid kit.
3	Put on personal protective equipment if appropriate.
4	If a child is hit hard in the eye or if an object punctures the eye, seek emergency help and call the parent/guardian. For a puncture, cover the eye with a clean, dry dressing. Tell the child to keep both eyes closed until trained help arrives and takes over.
5	If the eye is not punctured and a chemical or small irritant (such as eyelashes or sand) is in the eye, use running water from a faucet to rinse the irritant from the eye. Make sure the eye with the irritant is the lower eye as you rinse the eyes (see Figure 31 on page 84). Make sure you do not rinse the irritant into the unaffected eye.
6	If the object does not come out, or if the child complains about extreme pain, phone the parent/guardian or healthcare provider. Tell the child to keep both eyes closed until trained help arrives and takes over.

Fevers

What You Will Learn

By the end of this section you should be able to list the first aid actions for fever.

Actions for Fever

Fever is the body's natural way of fighting illness.

Follow these steps for fever:

Step	Action
1	Send someone to get the first aid kit.
2	Move the child away from any other children to lessen the chances of other children becoming ill.
3	Check the child's temperature.
4	Call the parent/guardian or healthcare provider if a child has a fever.
5	Give medicine to reduce fever if the child's parent/guardian or healthcare provider tells you to do so.

Do Not

Do not give aspirin to a child unless a healthcare provider tells you to do so.

FYI: Taking Temperature

There are different types of thermometers and different ways of taking temperature. It is not recommended that you use a mercury thermometer or take a rectal temperature.

Snake, Poisonous Spider, Scorpion, Tick, and Marine Animal Bites and Stings

What You Will Learn

By the end of this section you should be able to list the first aid actions for

- Snakebites
- Poisonous spider and scorpion bites
- Tick bites
- Marine animal bites

Type of Snake

If a snake bites a child, it is helpful to be able to identify the snake. Sometimes you can identify the snake from its bite mark or behavior. *If you aren't sure whether a snake is poisonous, assume that it is.*

The following lists the signs of poisonous snake bites:

- Progressive pain at the bite area
- Swelling of the bite area
- Nausea, vomiting, sweating, and weakness

**Actions for
Snakebites**

Follow these steps for a snakebite:

Step	Action
1	Be careful around a wounded snake. • Back away and go around the snake. • If a snake has been killed or hurt by accident, do not handle it. A snake might bite even when severely hurt or close to death. • If the snake needs to be moved, use a long-handled shovel. • If you don't need to move it, it is best to leave it alone.
2	Phone or send someone to phone your emergency response number (or 911) and bring the first aid kit.
3	Ask another adult to move any other children inside or away from the area.
4	Put on personal protective equipment if appropriate.
5	Ask the child to be still and calm.
6	Tell the child not to move the part of the body that was bitten.
7	Gently wash the bite area with running water (and soap if available).
8	If a coral snake bit the child, apply mild pressure by wrapping a bandage comfortably tight. You should still be able to slip or fit a finger under the bandage around the entire length of the arm or leg. *Note: Do not* wrap the bite area with a dressing if any other snake caused the bite.

Important
Snake bites can cause both pain and swelling. If a snake bites a child, remove any jewelry near the bite.

For information on coral snakes, refer to the CD.

Do Not
When you give first aid for snakebite • *Do not* apply cold or ice. • *Do not* apply suction. • *Do not* cut the wound. • *Do not* wrap the wound tightly. • *Do not* use local electric shock.

Signs of Poisonous Spider and Scorpion Bites and Stings

The following is a list of the signs of poisonous spider and scorpion bites and stings. Some of the signs may vary depending on the type of bite or sting.

- Severe pain at the site of the bite or sting
- Muscle cramps
- Headache
- Fever
- Vomiting
- Breathing problems
- Seizures
- The child does not respond

Actions for Spider Bites and Scorpion Bites and Stings

Follow these steps for a spider or scorpion bite or sting:

Actions for Nonpoisonous Spider and Other Bites and Stings	Actions for Poisonous Spider and Scorpion Bites and Stings
1. Wash the bite with running water (and soap if available). 2. Put an ice bag wrapped in a towel or cloth on the bite or sting.	1. Make sure the scene is safe for you and the child. 2. Phone your emergency response number (or 911) or poison control center immediately and get the first aid kit. 3. Wash the bite with running water (and soap if available). 4. Put an ice bag wrapped in a towel or cloth on the bite. 5. If the child stops responding, start the steps of CPR if you know how (see the section on CPR).

Ticks

Ticks are found on animals and in wooded areas. They attach themselves to exposed body parts. Many ticks are harmless. Some carry serious diseases, like Lyme disease.

If you find a tick (see Figure 32), remove it as soon as possible. The longer the tick stays attached to a child, the greater the child's chance of catching a disease.

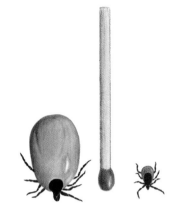

Figure 32. Left tick is engorged; match is for size.

Actions for Tick Bites

Follow these steps for a tick bite:

Step	Action
1	Grab the tick by its mouth or head as close to the skin as possible with a tweezers or tick-removing device. Try to avoid pinching the tick.
2	Lift the tick straight out without twisting or squeezing its body. If you lift the tick until the child's skin tents and wait for several seconds, the tick may let go.
3	Wash the bite with running water (and soap if available).
4	See a healthcare provider if you are in an area where Lyme disease occurs. If possible, place the tick in a plastic bag and give it to the healthcare provider.

Do Not

The following are the *wrong* actions to take when trying to remove a tick:

- *Do not* use petroleum jelly.
- *Do not* touch the tick with your bare hands.
- *Do not* use fingernail polish.
- *Do not* use rubbing alcohol.
- *Do not* use a hot match.
- *Do not* use gasoline.
- *Do not* twist or jerk the tick.

For a map of reported cases of Lyme disease in the United States, refer to the CD.

Marine Animal Bites and Stings

Marine fish and animals can bite or sting humans. Ocean bacteria may cause infection, so you must give first aid quickly.

If you live in an area with marine life, you must be prepared to give first aid for marine bites and stings. Also, if you have an aquarium in your office or school, you must know how to give first aid for marine animal bites and stings.

Actions for Marine Animal Bites and Stings

Follow these steps to give first aid to a child with a marine animal bite or sting:

Step	Action
1	Make sure that the scene is safe for you and the child. Do not touch any part of an animal that may be nearby.
2	Phone or send someone to phone your emergency response number (or 911) or poison control center and get the first aid kit.
3	Keep the child quiet and still.
4	Put on personal protective equipment if appropriate.
5	Wipe off stingers or tentacles with a towel. Do not touch them with your bare hands.
6	Rinse the bite or sting area with water. Use salt water if available.
7	Apply pressure to stop any bleeding.

Do Not

- *Do not* try to remove stingers without protecting your own hands.
- *Do not* give the child any medicine or put anything on the bite area unless a healthcare provider tells you to.

When to Call for Help

Phone your emergency response number (or 911) immediately if the child has

- Trouble breathing
- Bleeding you cannot stop
- Cramps
- Fever
- Sweating
- Weakness, faintness, or dizziness
- Upset stomach or vomiting
- Diarrhea
- Numbness or trouble moving part of the body

For more information on marine animal bites and stings, search for this topic on *www.medlineplus.gov.*

Suspected Abuse

What You Will Learn

By the end of this section you should be able to

- List the types of suspected abuse
- Tell the symptoms of abuse

Recognizing Suspected Abuse

Child abuse is any act that harms a child on purpose. The effects of abuse can last a lifetime. There are many types of abuse.

Type of Abuse	Definition
Physical Abuse	Actions toward a child that cause bodily injuries.
Emotional Abuse	Intentional words or behavior or lack of actions. These actions tell children that they are worthless, unloved, unwanted, in danger, or only of value to meet someone else's needs. Withholding emotional support, isolation, and terrorizing a child are forms of emotional abuse.
Sexual Abuse	Any act with a child that is intended to sexually gratify an adult. Sexual abusers can be young or old, male or female, and usually are family members or acquaintances of the child. Sexual abuse by a stranger is relatively rare.
Neglect	Leaving children in situations where they are at risk of physical or mental harm.

Symptoms of Abuse

Abused or neglected children often show both physical and behavioral symptoms. However, children usually either cannot or will not talk about the problem. Occasionally children will report mistreatment to an adult they trust. You should take these conversations seriously and report them.

The following table lists behavioral and physical signs of possible abuse:

Behavioral Signs of Possible Abuse	Physical Signs of Possible Abuse

• Developmental delays
• Parental lack of interest in the child
• Low self-esteem, anxiety, depression, or attempted suicide
• Sudden change in school grades
• Problem or inappropriate behavior
• Sexual knowledge that is inappropriate for the child's age
• Fear of caregiver or guardian
	• Extremely low weight for the child's age
	• Injuries that do not match the story:
	  — Bruises
	  — Broken bones
	  — Burns
	  — Bleeding, cuts, punctures
	  — Bites

Filing a Suspected Abuse Report

Any time you suspect child abuse, you may be required to report it to law enforcement or Child Protective Services (CPS). Laws differ from state to state, so check with local law enforcement officials to find out whether you have to report and, if so, what information to report.

Most states require the following:

- Child's name, age, and address
- Primary caretaker's name and address
- Physical indicators observed
- Behavioral indicators observed
- Your name (or you may report anonymously in some states) and relationship, association, or involvement

The identity of a person making a report is confidential and may be disclosed only by order of the court or to a law enforcement officer for investigation purposes.

Persons acting in good faith who report or assist in an investigation are free from civil or criminal liability.

It is important to remember that the person reporting abuse is not responsible for determining if the circumstances meet the legal definition of abuse. That is the role of law enforcement and CPS.

 Check your state regulations for additional rules.

Question	Your Notes
1. *True or false:* You do not need to phone your emergency response number (or 911) if an object punctures a child's eye. Circle your answer: True False	
2. *True or false:* If a child feels warm or has a fever, the child can continue to play with other children until the parent picks her up at the end of the day. Circle your answer: True False	
3. *True or false:* Signs of a poisonous spider bite include muscle cramps, head-ache, and fever. Circle your answer: True False	
4. *True or false:* A child who has low self-esteem, a sudden change in school grades or behavior, or sexual knowledge that is inappropriate for age may be a victim of possible child abuse. Circle your answer: True False	

CPR and AED

Adult CPR

What You Will Learn

By the end of this section you should be able to give CPR to an adult.

Ages for Adult CPR

Adult CPR is for victims 8 year of age and older.

Overview

If you know *when* to phone your emergency response number (or 911) and *how* to give compressions and breaths, your actions may save a life. In this course you will learn the basic steps of CPR first. Then you will put these steps together in order.

There are basic steps in giving CPR:

- Doing compressions
- Giving breaths that make the chest rise

Compressions

One of the most important parts of adult CPR is compressions. When you give compressions, you pump blood to the brain and heart. You will learn more about where compressions fit in the sequence of CPR later.

Actions for Compressions

Follow these steps to give compressions to adults:

Step	Action
1	Kneel at the victim's side.
2	Make sure the victim is lying on his back on a firm, flat surface. If the victim is lying facedown, carefully roll him onto his back.
3	Quickly move or remove clothes from the front of the chest that will get in the way of doing compressions and using an AED.
4	Put the heel of one hand on the center of the victim's chest between the nipples (Figure 33A). Put the heel of your other hand on top of the first hand (Figure 33B).
5	Push straight down on the chest 1½ to 2 inches with each compression. Push hard and fast.
6	Push at a rate of 100 compressions a minute.
7	After each compression, release pressure on the chest to let it come back to its normal position.

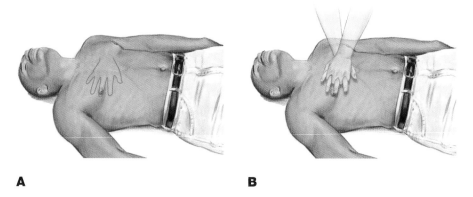

A   **B**

Figure 33. Chest compressions. **A,** Put the heel of one hand on the center of the chest between the nipples. **B,** Put the other hand on top of the first hand.

> ### *Important*
>
> - Push hard and push fast.
> - Push at a rate of 100 times a minute.
> - After each compression, release pressure on the chest to let it come back to its normal position.

Open the Airway

When giving CPR you must give the victim breaths that make the chest rise. Before giving breaths, you must open the airway with the head tilt–chin lift.

Performing the Head Tilt–Chin Lift

Follow these steps to perform a head tilt–chin lift (Figure 34):

Step	Action
1	Tilt the head by pushing back on the forehead.
2	Lift the chin by putting your fingers on the bony part of the chin. Do not press the soft tissues of the neck or under the chin.
3	Lift the chin to move the jaw forward.

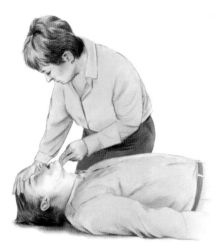

Figure 34. Open the airway with a head tilt–chin lift.

Giving Breaths

Your breaths give oxygen to someone who cannot breathe on his own.

Actions for Giving Breaths

Follow these steps to give breaths:

Step	Action
1	Hold the airway open with a head tilt–chin lift (Figure 34).
2	Pinch the nose closed.
3	Take a normal breath and cover the victim's mouth with your mouth, creating an airtight seal (Figure 35).
4	Give 2 breaths (blow for 1 second each). Watch for chest rise as you give each breath.

Figure 35. Give 2 breaths.

Compressions and Breaths	When you give CPR, you do sets of 30 compressions and 2 breaths. Try not to interrupt chest compressions for more than a few seconds. For example, don't take too long to give breaths or use the AED. Now you will learn how to give compressions and breaths in the right order.
Putting It All Together	You have learned compression and breaths. To put it all together in the right order, follow these steps.
Make Sure the Scene Is Safe	Before you give CPR, make sure the scene is safe for you and the victim (Figure 36). For example, make sure there is no traffic in the area that could injure you. You do not want to become a victim yourself.

Figure 36. Make sure the scene is safe.

Checking for Response

Check to see if the victim responds before giving CPR. Kneel at the victim's side. Tap the victim and shout, "Are you OK?" (Figure 37).

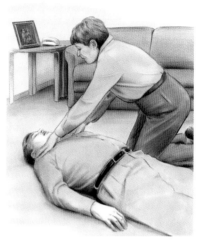

Figure 37. Check for response.

Getting Help

If the victim does not respond, it is important to get help on the way as soon as possible. Follow these steps to call for help:

Step	Action
1	If the victim does not respond, yell for help. If someone comes, send that person to phone your emergency response number (or 911) and get the AED if available.
2	If no one comes, leave the victim to phone your emergency response number (or 911) and get the AED if available (Figure 38). Return to the victim and start the steps of CPR.

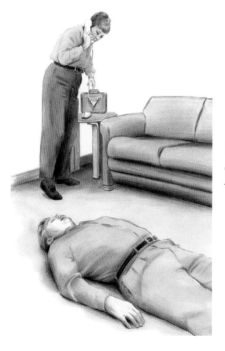

Figure 38. Get help. Phone your emergency response number (or 911) and get the AED if available.

Check Breathing

Once you have checked the victim for a response, you must check to see if the victim is breathing normally.

Step	Action
1	Open the victim's airway with a head tilt–chin lift.
2	Check to see if the victim is breathing normally (take at least 5 seconds but no more than 10 seconds) (Figure 39). • Put your ear next to the victim's mouth and nose. • **Look** to see if the chest rises. • **Listen** for breaths. • **Feel** for breaths on your cheek.

Figure 39. Look, listen, and feel for normal breathing.

Special Situations

Gasps Are Not Breaths

In the first few minutes after sudden cardiac arrest, a victim may only gasp.

Gasping is *not* breathing.

> **Important**
>
> If the victim gasps when you open the airway to check breathing, continue the steps of CPR. The victim is likely to need all the steps of CPR.

If the First Breath Does Not Go In

If you give a victim a breath and it does not go in, you will need to re-open the airway with a head tilt–chin lift before giving the second breath. After you give 2 breaths, you will give 30 compressions. You will repeat the sets of 30 compressions and 2 breaths until the AED arrives, the victim starts to move, or trained help arrives and takes over. Trained help could be someone whose job is taking care of people who are ill or injured such as an EMS responder, nurse, or doctor.

Side Position

If the victim is breathing normally but is not responding, roll the victim to his side and wait for trained help to take over (Figure 40). Placing a victim in the side position helps keep the airway open. If the victim stops moving again, you will need to start the steps of CPR from the beginning.

Figure 40. Side position.

Summary of Steps for Adult CPR

The following table summarizes the steps for adult CPR:

Step	Action
1	Make sure the scene is safe.
2	Make sure the victim is lying on his back on a firm, flat surface. If the victim is lying facedown, carefully roll him onto his back.
3	Kneel at the victim's side. Tap and shout to see if the victim responds.
4	If the victim does not respond, yell for help. • If someone comes, send that person to phone your emergency response number (or 911) and get the AED if available. • If no one comes, leave the victim to phone your emergency response number (or 911) and get the AED if available. After you answer all the dispatcher's questions, return to the victim and start the steps of CPR.
5	Open the airway with a head tilt–chin lift.
6	Check to see if the victim is breathing normally (take at least 5 seconds but no more than 10 seconds). • Put your ear next to the victim's mouth and nose. • **Look** to see if the chest rises. • **Listen** for breaths. • **Feel** for breaths on your cheek.
7	If there is no normal breathing, give 2 breaths (1 second each). Watch for chest rise as you give each breath.
8	Quickly move or remove clothes from the front of the chest that will get in the way of doing compressions and using an AED.
9	Give 30 compressions at a rate of 100 a minute and then give 2 breaths. After each compression, release pressure on the chest to let it come back to its normal position.
10	Keep giving sets of 30 compressions and 2 breaths until the AED arrives, the victim starts to move, or trained help arrives and takes over.

1. The correct rate for giving compressions is _____ compressions a minute.

2. For adult CPR you give sets of _____ compressions and _____ breaths.

3. When giving CPR how long should each breath take?
   a. 1 second
   b. 3 seconds
   c. 4 seconds

Child CPR

What You Will Learn

By the end of this section you should be able to give CPR to a child.

Ages for Child CPR

For purposes of this course, a child is 1 to 8 years of age.

Overview

While some steps for giving CPR to an adult and child are similar, there are a few differences:

- When to phone your emergency response number (or 911)
- Amount of air for breaths
- Depth of compressions
- Number of hands for compressions

When to Phone Your Emergency Response Number (or 911)

If you are alone, do 5 sets of 30 compressions and 2 breaths **before** leaving the child to phone your emergency response number (or 911). This is different from adult CPR, where you phone first.

Amount of Air for Breaths

Breaths are very important for children who do not respond. When giving breaths to children, be sure to open the airway and give breaths that make the chest rise, just as for adults. For small children you will not need to use the same amount of air for breaths as for larger children or adults. However, each breath should still make the chest rise.

Depth of Compressions

When you push on a child's chest, press straight down ⅓ to ½ the depth of the chest (Figure 41).

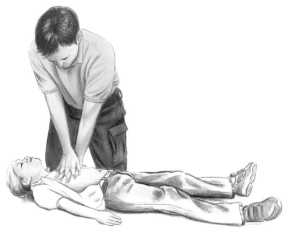

Figure 41. Two-handed compressions.

Number of Hands for Compressions

You may need to use only one hand for compressions for very small children (Figure 42). Whether you use 1 hand or 2 hands, it is important to be sure to push straight down ⅓ to ½ the depth of the chest.

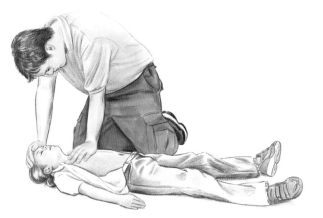

Figure 42. One-handed compressions.

Summary of Steps for Child CPR

The following table shows the steps for giving CPR to a child 1 to 8 years of age.

Step	Action
1	Make sure the scene is safe.
2	Make sure the victim is lying on her back on a firm, flat surface. If the victim is lying facedown, carefully roll her onto her back.
3	Kneel at the victim's side. Tap and shout to see if the victim responds.
4	If the victim does not respond, yell for help. • If someone comes, send that person to phone your emergency response number (or 911) and get the AED if available. • If no one comes, stay with the child and start the steps of CPR.
5	Open the airway with a head tilt–chin lift.
6	Check to see if the victim is breathing (take at least 5 seconds but no more than 10 seconds). • Put your ear next to the victim's mouth and nose. • **Look** to see if the chest rises. • **Listen** for breaths. • **Feel** for breaths on your cheek.
7	If the child is not breathing, give 2 breaths (1 second each). Watch for chest rise as you give each breath.
8	Quickly move or remove clothes from the front of the chest that will get in the way of doing compressions and using an AED.
9	Give 30 compressions at a rate of 100 a minute and then give 2 breaths. After each compression, release pressure on the chest to let it come back to its normal position.
10	After 5 sets of 30 compressions and 2 breaths, if someone has not done this, phone your emergency response number (or 911) and get an AED if available.
11	After you answer all of the dispatcher's questions, return to the child and start the steps of CPR.
12	Keep giving sets of 30 compressions and 2 breaths until an AED arrives, the victim starts to move, or trained help takes over.

Special Situations

When giving CPR to children 1 to 8 years of age, you handle special situations, such as re-opening the airway if the first breath does not go in and the side position, the same way as you do for adults.

Review Questions

1. When giving compressions to a child, press down _____ to _____ the depth of the chest.

2. True or false: If you are alone with a child who does not respond, you should give 5 sets of 30 compressions and 2 breaths before phoning your emergency response number (or 911).

Use of Mask–Adult/Child

Using a Mask

During CPR there is very little chance that you will catch a disease. Some regulatory agencies, including the Occupational Safety and Health Administration (OSHA), require that certain rescuers use a mask when giving breaths in the workplace (Figure 43). You may also want to use a mask or other barrier device when giving CPR to victims outside the workplace who are not family members.

Masks are made of firm plastic and fit over the victim's mouth or mouth and nose. You may need to put the mask together before you use it.

Figure 43. Mask for giving breaths.

Actions for Giving Breaths With a Mask

Follow these steps to give breaths using a mask:

Step	Action
1	Kneel at the victim's side.
2	Put the mask over the victim's mouth and nose.
3	Tilt the head and lift the chin while pressing the mask against the victim's face. It is important to make an airtight seal between the victim's face and the mask while you lift the chin to keep the airway open.
4	Give 2 breaths. Watch for chest rise as you give each breath (Figure 44).

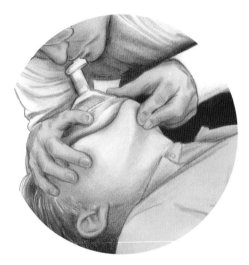

Figure 44. Giving breaths with a mask.

FYI: Masks With Pointed Ends

If the mask has a pointed end

- Put the narrow end of the mask at the top (bridge) of the nose.
- The wide end should cover the mouth.

**What You
Will Learn**

By the end of this section you should be able to

- Tell what an AED does
- Tell when you might use an AED
- List the steps for using an AED
- Tell how to give CPR and use an AED

Overview

AEDs are accurate and easy to use. After very little training, most people can operate an AED. Giving CPR right away and using an AED within a few minutes will increase the chances of saving the life of someone with sudden cardiac arrest.

**What an
AED Does**

An automated external defibrillator (AED) is a machine with a computer inside (Figure 45). An AED can

- Recognize cardiac arrest that requires a shock
- Tell the rescuer when a shock is needed
- Give a shock if needed

An AED may give an electric shock to the heart. This can stop the abnormal heart rhythm and allow a normal heart rhythm to return.

The AED will use visual and audible prompts to tell the rescuer the steps to take. There are many different brands of AEDs, but the same simple steps operate all of them.

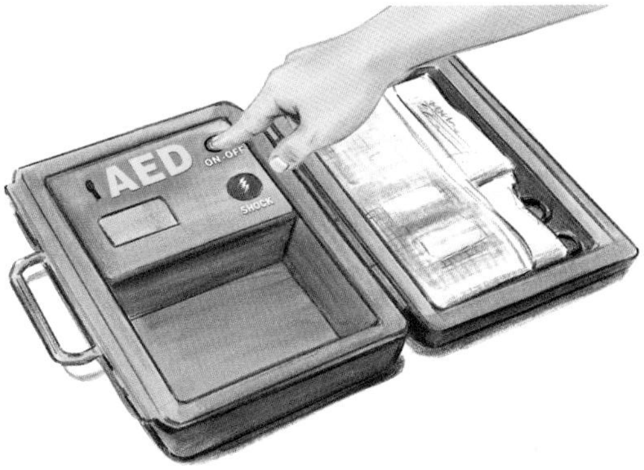

Figure 45. An automated external defibrillator (AED).

When You Might Use an AED

A victim who does not respond may have an abnormal heart rhythm that stops the heart from pumping blood. You will use an AED on a victim aged 1 and older only when that victim does not respond and is not breathing.

- For victims 8 years of age and older, start CPR right away and use an AED as soon as it is available.

- For victims 1 to 8 years of age, perform 5 sets of 30 compressions and 2 breaths or about 2 minutes of CPR before attaching and using the AED.

FYI: AEDs and Infants

There is currently not enough data for the AHA to recommend for or against using AEDs in infants less than approximately 1 year of age.

FYI: AED Pads

Some AEDs can deliver a smaller shock dose for children if you use child pads or a child key or switch. If the AED can deliver this smaller shock dose, use it for children 1 to 8 years of age. If the AED cannot give a child dose, you can use the adult pads (Figure 46A) and give an adult shock dose for children 1 to 8 years of age.

For victims 8 years of age and older, always use the larger adult pads and adult dose—DO NOT use child pads (Figure 46B) or a child dose for a victim 8 years of age and older. You should know how to operate the AED in your workplace and know if it can provide a child dose and how to deliver that dose for a child.

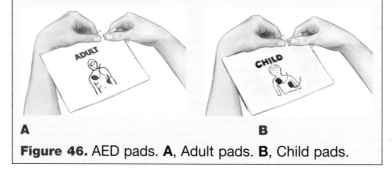

A   **B**

Figure 46. AED pads. **A**, Adult pads. **B**, Child pads.

Steps for Using an AED

Use the same simple steps to operate all AEDs:

Step	Action
1	**Turn the AED on.** Push the button or open the lid (Figure 47). Follow the visual and audible prompts.
2	**Attach pads** (Figure 48).
3	**Allow the AED to check the heart rhythm.** Make sure no one touches the victim (Figure 49).
4	**Push the SHOCK button if the AED tells you to do so (Figure 50).** Make sure no one touches the victim. If a shock is delivered, start the steps of CPR right after shock delivery.

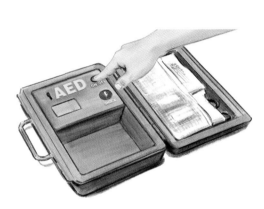

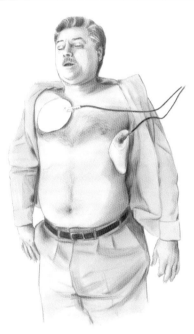

Figure 47. Turn on the AED.

Figure 48. Attach pads.

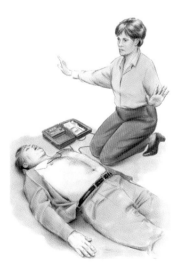

Figure 49. Make sure no one is touching the victim.

Figure 50. Be sure no one tourches the victim, and press SHOCK if needed.

Use the AED fast. For adult victims time from arrival of the AED to first shock should be less than 90 seconds.

If the AED does not tell you to give a shock, follow the AED visual and audible prompts. Be ready to resume CPR if needed.

Attaching Pads

Follow these steps when attaching pads:

Step	Action
1	Choose the correct pad (adult vs child) for size/age of victim.
2	Open the AED pad package and peel away the plastic backing.
3	Attach the sticky side of the pads directly to the victim's bare chest (Figure 48). The picture on the pad will show you where to put the pads.

Clearing the Victim

You must "clear" the victim before the AED analyzes the victim's heart rhythm or gives a shock dose to the victim. To clear the victim, look around to make sure no one touches the victim when the AED prompts you to clear.

Special Situations

Special situations will change the way you use an AED.

Water
Do not deliver a shock when a victim is

- Lying in water
- Covered with water (for example, the victim is covered with sweat or has just been pulled from a swimming pool)

Water may cause the shock to flow over the skin from one pad to the other. If that happens, energy won't go to the heart.

If you give a shock in water, the AED also might shock the rescuer.

Step	Action
1	Move the victim away from standing water.
2	Quickly wipe the victim's chest before you attach the pads.

> **FYI: AEDs and Small Amounts of Water**
>
> If the victim is lying in a small puddle of water or snow but the chest is not covered with water, you can give shocks.

Medicine Patch

You should not put an AED pad over a medicine patch. The patch may block some of the shock dose so that some of the energy does not reach the heart. Also, giving a shock over the patch may burn the victim.

Step	Action
1	If a child or adult has a medicine patch in the same place where you would attach the AED pad, take the medicine patch off while wearing gloves.
2	Quickly wipe the chest where the patch was before you put on the pad.

Implanted Pacemaker or Defibrillator

Some children or adults may have an implanted pacemaker or defibrillator. These devices make a hard lump under the skin of the chest or in the abdomen. The lump is smaller than a deck of cards. You should not put an AED pad over this lump because the implanted device may block delivery of the shock to the heart.

Step	Action
1	Look for a lump under the skin of the chest that looks smaller than a deck of cards.
2	If you see this lump where the pads should go, put the pads at least 1 inch away from the lump.

Hairy Chest

If a victim has a hairy chest, the AED pads may stick to the hair instead of the skin on the chest. If this happens, the AED will not be able to check the victim's heart rhythm or deliver a shock. The AED will prompt you to check the pads.

Step	Action
1	If the pads stick to the hair instead of the skin, press down firmly on each pad.
2	If the AED still tells you to check the pads, quickly pull off the pads to remove the hair.
3	If a lot of hair still remains where you will put the pads, shave the area with the razor in the AED carrying case.
4	Put on a new set of pads. Follow the AED visible and audible prompts.

FYI: AEDs in the Community

The American Heart Association supports placing AEDs throughout the community in lay rescuer AED programs. AEDs are placed in many public places where large numbers of people gather, such as sports stadiums, airports, airplanes, and an increasing number of worksites.

AED programs usually are directed by a healthcare provider and are linked with the local EMS system. AED rescuers, such as police, security guards, lifeguards, and other first aid providers should be trained in CPR and the use of an AED.

You can increase the chance of survival for a victim of sudden cardiac arrest if you give the victim CPR right away and use an AED within a few minutes.

Notes

You can get the answers for these items at your workplace after the course.

Key Points From My Workplace Emergency Response Policies and Procedures

How to access the workplace emergency response system:

Phone _____

Where the AED is located: _____

What changes do you need to make to use the AED on a child?

____Use "child" pads

____Insert a "child" key or turn a "child" switch

____Other: _____

Masks used at the workplace (check one):

____Yes ____ No

Other Key Points:

_____

_____

_____

1. True or false: You can use adult AED pads on a child if child pads are not available.

2. Which of the following best describes "clearing the victim"?

    a. Taking the pads off the victim's chest

    b. Making sure no one is touching the victim

    c. Moving the victim to a clear room

Infant CPR

What You Will Learn

By the end of this section you should be able to give CPR to an infant.

Ages for Infant CPR

Infant CPR is for victims from birth to 1 year of age.

Overview

Although some steps for giving CPR to an infant are similar to giving CPR to an adult or child, there are a few differences:

- How to give compressions
- How to open the airway
- How to give breaths
- How to use a mask
- How to check for response

You will first learn these skills of CPR for the infant that are different from adult and child CPR. Then you will learn to put all the steps together in the correct order.

Compressions

As with CPR for the adult and child, compressions are a very important part of infant CPR. Compressions pump blood to the brain and heart.

Actions for Compressions

Follow these steps to give compressions to an infant:

Step	Action
1	Place the infant on a firm, flat surface. If possible, place the infant on a surface above the ground, such as a table. This makes it easier to give CPR to the infant.
2	Quickly move or open clothes from the front of the chest that will get in the way of doing compressions.
3	Put 2 fingers of one hand just below the nipple line. Do not put your fingers over the very bottom of the breastbone (Figure 51).
4	Press the infant's breastbone straight down ⅓ to ½ *the depth* of the chest. Push hard and fast.
5	Repeat at a rate of 100 compressions per minute.
6	After each compression, release pressure on the chest to let it come back to its normal position.

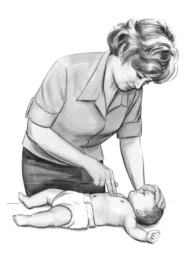

Figure 51. Pushing on the chest. Put 2 fingers just below the nipple line.

Important

- Push hard and push fast.
- Push at a rate of 100 times a minute.
- After each compression, release pressure on the chest to let it come back to its normal position.

Open the Airway

When giving CPR you must give the infant breaths that make the chest rise. Before giving breaths you must open the airway with the head tilt–chin lift.

Performing the Head Tilt–Chin Lift

When you open an infant's airway, use the head tilt–chin lift (Figure 52). When tilting an infant's head, do not push it back too far because it may block the infant's airway.

Giving Breaths

Breaths are very important for infants who are not breathing or do not respond. Your breaths give an infant oxygen when the infant cannot breathe on his own. You will not have to give as large a breath to an infant as you give to a child or an adult.

Actions for Giving Breaths

Follow these steps to give breaths to infants:

Step	Action
1	Hold the infant's airway open with a head tilt–chin lift (Figure 52).
2	Take a normal breath and cover the infant's mouth and nose with your mouth, creating an airtight seal (Figure 53).
3	Give 2 breaths (blow for 1 second each). Watch for chest rise as you give each breath.

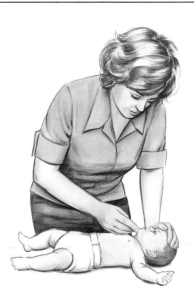

Figure 52. Use the head tilt-chin lift.

Figure 53. Cover the infant's mouth and nose with your mouth.

119

> ### *FYI: Tips for Giving Breaths*
>
> If your mouth is too small to cover the infant's mouth and nose, put your mouth over the infant's nose and give breaths through the infant's nose. (You may need to hold the infant's mouth closed to prevent air from escaping through the mouth.)

Check for Response

Check to see if the infant responds before giving CPR. Tap the infant's foot and shout, "Are you OK?" (Figure 54).

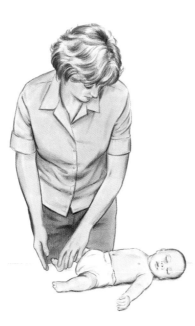

Figure 54. Check for response.

Get Help

If the infant does not respond, it is important to get help on the way as soon as possible. Follow these steps to get help:

Step	Action
1	If the infant does not respond, yell for help. If someone comes, send that person to phone your emergency response number (or 911).
2	If no one comes, stay with the infant and continue the steps of CPR.

Special Situation

If you give an infant a breath and it does not go in, you will need to re-open the airway with a head tilt–chin lift before giving the second breath.

Summary of Steps for Infant CPR

The following table summarizes the steps for infant CPR:

Step	Action
1	Make sure the scene is safe.
2	Tap the infant's foot and shout to see if the infant responds.
3	If the infant does not respond, yell for help. • If someone comes, send that person to phone your emergency response number (or 911). • If no one comes, stay with the infant to start the steps of CPR.
4	Place the infant on a firm, flat surface. If possible, place the infant on a surface above the ground, such as a table.
5	Open the airway with a head tilt–chin lift.
6	Check to see if the infant is breathing (take at least 5 seconds but no more than 10 seconds). • Put your ear next to the infant's mouth and nose. • **Look** to see if the chest rises. • **Listen** for breaths. • **Feel** for breaths on your cheek.
7	If the infant is not breathing, give 2 breaths (1 second each). Watch for chest rise as you give each breath.
8	Quickly move or open clothes from the front of the chest that will get in the way of doing compressions.
9	Give 30 compressions at a rate of 100 a minute and then give 2 breaths. After each compression, release pressure on the chest to let it come back to its normal position.
10	After 5 sets of 30 compressions and 2 breaths, if someone has not already phoned, leave the infant and phone your emergency response number (or 911).
11	After you answer all of the dispatcher's questions, return to the infant and start the steps of CPR.
12	Keep giving sets of 30 compressions and 2 breaths until the infant starts to move or trained help arrives and takes over.

> **FYI: Taking the Infant With You to Phone for Help**
>
> If the infant is not injured and you are alone, after 5 sets of 30 compressions and 2 breaths, you may carry the infant with you to phone your emergency response number (or 911).

Using a Mask

Using a mask for an infant is the same as for an adult or child except for a couple of things:

- Any mask should cover the infant's nose and mouth but should not cover the infant's eyes.
- If you do not have an infant mask, follow the recommendations of the manufacturer of the mask you are using.

Review Questions

1. The correct rate for giving compressions is _____ compressions a minute.

2. For infant CPR you give sets of _____ compressions and _____ breaths.

3. When giving CPR to an infant, how long should each breath take?

   a. 1 second
   b. 3 seconds
   c. 4 seconds

Conclusion

Congratulations on taking time to attend this course. Contact the American Heart Association if you want more information on CPR, AEDs, or even first aid. You can visit *www.americanheart.org/cpr* or call 877-AHA-4CPR (877-242-4277) to find a class near you.

Even if you don't remember all the steps of CPR exactly, it is important for you to try. And always remember to phone your emergency response number (or 911). They can remind you what to do.

Comparison of CPR and AED Steps for Adults, Children, and Infants

CPR	Adult and Older Child (8 Years of Age and Older)	Child (1 to 8 Years Old)	Infant (Less Than 1 Year Old)
Check for response	Tap and shout		Tap the infant's foot and shout
Phone your emergency response number (or 911)	Phone your emergency response number (or 911) as soon as you find that the victim does not respond	Phone your emergency response number (or 911) after giving 5 sets of 30 compressions and 2 breaths	
Open the airway Use head tilt–chin lift	Head tilt–chin lift		Head tilt–chin lift (do not tilt head back too far)
Check breathing If the victim is not breathing, give 2 breaths that make the chest rise	Open the airway, look, listen, and feel (Take at least 5 seconds but no more than 10 seconds)		
First 2 breaths	Give 2 breaths (1 second each)		
Start CPR	Give sets of 30 compressions and 2 breaths		
• **Compression location**	Center of chest between nipples		Just below the nipple line
• **Compression method**	2 hands	1 or 2 hands	2 fingers
• **Compression depth**	1½ to 2 inches	⅓ to ½ depth of chest	
• **Compression rate**	100 a minute		
• **Sets of compressions and breaths**	30:2		
To relieve choking	Abdominal thrusts		Back slaps and chest thrusts (no abdominal thrusts)
AED • **Turn the power on (or open the case)**	Use AED as soon as it arrives	Use AED after 5 sets of 30 compressions and 2 breaths	
• **Attach pads to the victim's bare chest**	Use adult pads	Use child pads/key/switch or adult pads	
• **Allow the AED to check the heart rhythm**	Clear and analyze		
• **Push the SHOCK button if prompted by the AED**	Clear and shock		
• **Time from arrival of AED to first shock**	Less than 90 seconds		

Heartsaver Pediatric
First Aid Course
Adult/Child CPR and AED
Student Practice Sheet

American Heart
Association®

*Learn and Live*_{SM}

Step	Critical Performance Steps	Details
1	_____ Check for response	Tap victim and ask if the person is "all right" or "OK," speaking loudly and clearly.
2	_____ Tell someone to phone your emergency response number (or 911) and get an AED	Tell someone to perform **both** actions.
3	_____ Open airway using head tilt–chin lift	Place palm of one hand on forehead. Place fingers of other hand under the lower jaw to lift the chin. Obvious movement of the head back toward the hand on the forehead.
4	_____ Check breathing	Place face near the victim's nose and mouth to listen and feel for victim's breath. Look at chest. Take at least 5 seconds but no more than 10 seconds.
5	_____ Give 2 breaths (1 second each)	Seal your mouth over victim's mouth and blow. Your exhaled breaths should take 1 second each. Reposition the head if chest does not rise.
6	_____ Bare victim's chest and locate CPR hand position	Move or remove clothing from front of victim's chest. Place heel of one hand in the center of chest, between the nipples.
7	_____ Deliver first cycle of 30 compressions at the correct rate	Give 30 compressions in less than 23 seconds. Push hard; push fast; let chest return to normal between compressions.
8	_____ Give 2 breaths (1 second each)	Seal your mouth over victim's mouth and blow. Your exhaled breaths should take 1 second each. Reposition the head if chest does not rise.

PRACTICE SHEETS

Adult/Child CPR and AED Student Practice Sheet (continued)

Step	Critical Performance Steps	Details
AED Arrives		
AED 1	_____ Turn AED on	Stop CPR and press button to turn AED on (or make sure that AED case is open if your AED has an automatic-on feature).
AED 2	_____ Select proper pads and place pads correctly	Recognize the difference between adult pads and child pads: • Select the proper pad size for the manikin • Apply the pads to the chest as pad diagrams and/or AED instructions show
AED 3	_____ Clear victim to analyze	Show a visible sign of clearing the victim and a spoken indication of clearing the victim: "Clear! Stay clear of victim!" or similar words with an obvious gesture to make sure all are clear.
AED 4	_____ Clear victim to shock/press shock button	Show a visible sign of clearing the victim and a spoken indication of clearing the victim: "Clear! Stay clear of victim!" or similar words with an obvious gesture to make sure all are clear. Press shock button when prompted and after clearing. For adult victim, time from arrival of AED to first shock must be less than 90 seconds.
Continue CPR		
9	_____ Resume CPR: deliver second cycle of compressions using correct hand position	Place heel of one hand in the center of chest, between the nipples. Do 30 compressions. Push hard; push fast; let chest return to normal between compressions.
10	_____ Give 2 breaths (1 second each)	Seal your mouth over victim's mouth and blow. Your exhaled breaths should take 1 second each. Reposition the head if chest does not rise.
11	_____ Deliver third cycle of compressions of adequate depth with chest returning to normal	Do 30 compressions. Push hard; push fast; let chest return to normal between compressions.

Heartsaver Pediatric First Aid Course
Infant CPR
Student Practice Sheet

American Heart Association®

*Learn and Live*sm

Step	Critical Performance Steps	Details
1	_____ Check for response	Tap infant's foot and shout loudly.
2	_____ Tell someone to phone your emergency response number (or 911)	Tell someone to phone emergency response number (or 911). (During class practice there is someone to phone 911; otherwise do 2 minutes of CPR before phoning 911.)
3	_____ Open airway using head tilt–chin lift	Push back on forehead, place fingers on the bony part of the victim's chin and lift the victim's chin. Do not press the neck or under the chin. Lift the jaw upward by bringing the chin forward. Do not push the head back too far.
4	_____ Check breathing	Place face near the victim's nose and mouth to listen and feel for victim's breath. Look at chest. Take at least 5 seconds but no more than 10 seconds.
5	_____ Give 2 breaths (1 second each) with visible chest rise	Seal your mouth over victim's nose and mouth and blow. Your exhaled breaths should take 1 second each. You should be able to see the chest rise twice.
6	_____ Bare victim's chest and locate CPR finger position	Move or open clothing from front of victim's chest. Place 2 fingers just below the nipple line.
7	_____ Deliver first cycle of 30 compressions at the correct rate	Give 30 compressions in less than 23 seconds. Push hard; push fast; let chest return to normal between compressions.
8	_____ Give 2 breaths (1 second each) with visible chest rise	Seal your mouth over victim's nose and mouth and blow. Your exhaled breaths should take 1 second each. You should be able to see the chest rise twice.
9	_____ Deliver second cycle of compressions using correct finger position	Compress chest with 2 fingers just below the nipple line. Do 30 compressions. Push hard; push fast; let chest return to normal between compressions.
10	_____ Give 2 breaths (1 second each) with visible chest rise	Seal your mouth over victim's nose and mouth and blow. Your exhaled breaths should take 1 second each. You should be able to see the chest rise twice.
11	_____ Deliver third cycle of compressions of adequate depth with chest returning to normal	Do 30 compressions. Push hard; push fast; let chest return to normal between compressions.

Heartsaver Pediatric First Aid
Course Evaluation

American Heart
Association®

Learn and Live sm

Our goal is to ensure that we are providing an effective program that meets your needs and expectations. We value your opinion and need your feedback. Please take a moment to complete this course evaluation. The administrator of this program will review your ratings and comments on the delivery, facilities, instructor, and overall satisfaction with the course.

Administration and Facilities

Date of course? _____ Who were the instructors? _____

Where was the course held? _____

Circle a number that matches your opinion on each statement.

	Strongly Disagree	Disagree	Neutral	Agree	Strongly Agree
It was easy to enroll in the course.	1	2	3	4	5
I received my *Heartsaver Student Workbook* and CD in time for me to read the pre-class assignments.	1	2	3	4	5
The course facilities were adequate.	1	2	3	4	5
There was enough equipment available for everyone to practice skills with little "standing around" time.	1	2	3	4	5
The equipment was clean and in good working order.	1	2	3	4	5

Instruction

Circle a number that matches your opinion on each statement.

	Strongly Disagree	Disagree	Neutral	Agree	Strongly Agree
My instructor communicated clearly.	1	2	3	4	5
My instructor answered my questions.	1	2	3	4	5

Satisfaction

Circle a number that matches your opinion on each statement.

	Strongly Disagree	Disagree	Neutral	Agree	Strongly Agree
I would recommend this course to others.	1	2	3	4	5
I can apply the skills I learned.	1	2	3	4	5

Any comments you would like to make on the delivery, facilities, instructor, and overall satisfaction with the course? Please write your comments on the back of this form.

Please return your completed course evaluation to your instructor or your regional ECC office.

Child and Infant Safety Checklist

The Safety Checklist can help you learn risks for injury at home, in the car, at childcare centers, at schools, and on playgrounds. The Safety Checklist also tells you what to do to reduce risk. It is impossible to eliminate every risk for every child. For this reason, you must know how to respond to an emergency.

Action	I follow this safety precaution (✔ = yes)	Purchase of safety item is required for all shaded boxes (✔ = item purchased)
Car Safety		
1. Make sure that every person in the car "buckles up" correctly.		
2. Have children who are less than 12 years old ride in the BACK seat and use correct child restraints or lap-shoulder restraints for age.		
3. Use a rear-facing infant safety seat for infants until they weigh at least 20 lb (9 kg) and are 1 year old. ■ Secure all car seats in the BACK seat of the car. ■ Secure the seat according to the manufacturer's instructions. ■ To see if the seat is secure, try to push the seat forward, backward, and side-to-side. Tighten the belt to be sure that the seat does not move more than ½ inch (1 cm). ■ For proper adjustment, the seat belt buckle and latch plate (if needed) must be located well below the frame or toward the center of the seat.		☐ **Safety item— Infant safety seat**
4. Wait until a child weighs 20 lb (9 kg) and is at least 1 year old and can sit with good head control before using a convertible seat or toddler seat in the forward-facing position. Secure these seats in the BACK seat of the car.		☐ **Safety item— Child safety seat**
5. Use a belt-positioning booster seat for children who weigh 40 to 80 lb (18 to 36 kg). Secure the seat with a 3-point seat belt (lap and shoulder belt) in the BACK seat of the car. ■ If a shield is provided, fasten it close to the child's body. ■ Properly install the tether harness if required.		☐ **Safety item— Belt-positioning booster seat**
6. Children cannot be properly restrained with a lap-shoulder belt until they are at least 4 feet 9 inches (58 inches or 148 cm) tall, weigh 80 lb (36 kg), and can sit in the automobile seat with their knees bent over the edge. Always use a combination lap-shoulder belt to restrain children sitting in an automobile seat. ■ The shoulder belt should fit across the shoulder and breastbone. If it crosses the child's face and neck, use a belt-positioning booster seat to be sure that the belt is properly placed. Do not hook the shoulder belt under the child's arm. ■ All children 12 years old or younger should ride in the BACK seat.		

Action	I follow this safety precaution (✔ = yes)	Purchase of safety item is required for all shaded boxes (✔ = item purchased)
General Indoor Safety		
7. Place a sticker with emergency phone numbers near or on the phone. Include numbers for the EMS system, police, fire department, local hospital or physician, the poison control center in your area, and your telephone number.		☐ Safety item— **Phone sticker with emergency response numbers**
8. Install smoke detectors on the ceiling in the hallway outside areas where children sleep or nap and on each floor at the head of stairs. Test the alarm monthly and replace batteries twice a year (for example, in the fall and spring when the time changes to and from daylight saving time).		☐ Safety item— **Smoke detector**
9. Make sure that there are two unobstructed emergency exits from the home, childcare center, classroom, or other area where children are likely to be present.		
10. Develop and practice a fire escape plan.		
11. Make sure that a working fire extinguisher is available.		☐ Safety item— **Fire extinguisher**
12. Make sure that all space heaters are safety approved. They should be in safe operating condition. They should be placed out of a child's reach and at least 3 feet from curtains, papers, and furniture. The heaters should have protective covers.		
13. Make sure all wood-burning stoves are inspected yearly and vented properly. Place stoves out of a child's reach.		
14. Make sure that electrical cords are not frayed or overloaded. Place out of a child's reach.		
15. Install "shock stops" (plastic outlet plugs) or outlet covers on all electrical outlets.		☐ Safety item— **Plastic outlet plugs**
16. To prevent falls, always keep one hand on an infant sitting or lying on a high surface such as a changing table.		
17. Place healthy full-term infants on their back or side to sleep. Do not place infants on their stomach to sleep.		
18. Make sure the crib is safe: ■ The crib mattress fits snugly with no more than two fingers' width between the mattress and crib railing. ■ The distance between crib slats should be less than 2 3/8 inches (so the infant's head won't be caught). ■ Do not put any fluffy material, stuffed animals, or fluffy blankets or comforters in the crib with the infant		
19. Be sure that stairs, railings, porches, and balconies are strong and in good repair.		

Action	I follow this safety precaution (✔ = yes)	Purchase of safety item is required for all shaded boxes (✔ = item purchased)
20. Keep halls and stairs lighted to prevent falls.		
21. Put toddler gates at the top and bottom of stairs. (Do not use accordion-type gates with wide spaces at the top. The child's head could become trapped in such a gate, and the child could strangle.)		☐ Safety item— Toddler gates (NOT accordion-type)
22. Do not let your child use an infant walker.		
23. To prevent falls, put locks (available at hardware stores) on all windows. Put gates on the lower part of open windows.		☐ Safety item— Window locks, gates
24. Store medicines and vitamins in child-resistant containers out of a child's reach.		☐ Safety item— Child-resistant containers
25. Store cleaning products out of a child's sight and reach. ■ Store and label all household poisons in their original containers in high locked cabinets (not under sinks). ■ Do not store chemicals or poisons in soda bottles. ■ Store cleaning products away from food.		
26. Install safety latches or locks on cabinets that contain potentially dangerous items and are within a child's reach.		☐ Safety item— Safety latches or locks on cabinets
27. Keep purses that contain vitamins, medicines, cigarettes, matches, jewelry, and calculators (which have easy-to-swallow button batteries) out of a child's reach.		
28. Install a lock or hook-and-eye latch on the door to the basement or garage to keep children from entering those areas. Put a lock at the top of the doorframe.		☐ Safety item— Latch on basement, garage doors
29. Keep plants that may be harmful out of a child's reach. (Many plants are poisonous. Check with your poison control center.)		
30. Make sure that toy chests have lightweight lids, no lids, or safe-closing hinges.		

Action	I follow this safety precaution (✔ = yes)	Purchase of safety item is required for all shaded boxes (✔ = item purchased)
Kitchen Safety		
31. To reduce the risk of burns: ■ Keep hot liquids, foods, and cooking utensils out of a child's reach. ■ Put hot liquids and food away from the edge of the table. ■ Cook on back burners when possible and turn pot handles toward the center of the stove. ■ Avoid using tablecloths and placemats that can be pulled, spilling hot liquids or food. ■ Keep high chairs and stools away from the stove. ■ Do not keep snacks near the stove. ■ Teach young children the meaning of the word *hot*.		
32. Keep all foods and small items (including balloons) that can choke a child out of reach. Test toys for size with a toilet-paper roll. If a toy can fit inside the roll, it can choke a small child.		
33. Keep knives and other sharp objects out of a child's reach.		
Bathroom Safety		
34. Bathe children in no more than 1 or 2 inches of water. Stay with infants and young children throughout bath time. Do not leave small infants or toddlers in the bathtub in the care of young siblings.		
35. Use skid-proof mats or stickers in the bathtub.		☐ Safety item—bath mats or stickers
36. Adjust the maximum temperature of the water heater to 120°F to 130°F (48.9°C to 54.4°C) or medium heat. Test temperature with a thermometer.		
37. Keep electrical appliances (radios, hairdryers, space heaters, etc) out of the bathroom or unplugged, away from water, and out of a child's reach.		
Firearms		
38. If firearms are stored in the home, keep them locked and out of a child's sight and reach. Lock and unload guns individually before storing them. Store ammunition separate from the firearms.		☐ Safety item—trigger lock, lockboxes for firearms

Action	I follow this safety precaution (✔ = yes)	Purchase of safety item is required for all shaded boxes (✔ = item purchased)
Outdoor Safety		
39. Make sure playground equipment is assembled and anchored correctly according to the manufacturer's instructions. The playground should have a level, cushioned surface such as sand or wood chips.		
40. Make sure your child knows the rules of safe bicycling: ■ Wear a protective helmet. ■ Use the correct-size bicycle. ■ Ride on the right side of the road (with traffic). ■ Use hand signals and wear bright or reflective clothing.		☐ **Safety item— Bicycle helmet**
41. Do not allow children to play with fireworks.		
42. Make sure your child is properly protected while roller skating or skateboarding: ■ Wear a helmet and protective pads on the knees and elbows. ■ Skate only in rinks or parks that are free of traffic.		☐ **Safety item— Helmet and protective padding**
43. Make sure your child is properly protected while riding on sleds or snow disks. ■ Sled only during daylight hours and only in a safe, supervised area away from motor vehicles.		
44. Make sure your child is properly protected while participating in contact sports: ■ Proper adult instruction and supervision are provided. ■ Teammates are about the same weight and size. ■ Appropriate safety equipment is used.		☐ **Safety item— Safety equipment for contact sports**
45. To reduce the risk of animal bites, teach your child ■ How to handle and care for a pet. ■ Never to try to separate fighting animals, even when a familiar pet is involved. ■ To avoid unfamiliar animals.		

Action	I follow this safety precaution (✔ = yes)	Purchase of safety item is required for all shaded boxes (✔ = item purchased)
46. If you have a home swimming pool, make sure the pool is totally enclosed with fencing that is at least 5 feet high and that all gates are self-closing and self-latching. There should be no direct access (without a locked gate) from the home into the pool area. In addition: ■ An adult must always supervise children while they swim. Never allow a child to swim alone. ■ Change young children from swimsuits into street clothes, and remove all toys from the pool area at the end of swim time. ■ All adults and older children should learn CPR. ■ Pools on nearby properties should be protected from use by unsupervised children.		☐ **Safety item— 5-foot fence around swimming pool with self-closing, self-latching gate**

Note: Much of the safety information presented in this table is based on the SAFEHOME program and the Children's Traffic Safety Program at Vanderbilt University in Nashville, Tennessee. The Massachusetts Department of Public Health developed the SAFEHOME program as part of its Statewide Comprehensive Injury Prevention Program. The Federal Division of Maternal and Child Health funded the SAFEHOME program. The Department of Transportation and the Tennessee Governor's Highway Safety Program funded the Children's Traffic Safety Program.

INDEX